Visual Discriminat

Look at each row of pictures. Circle each picture that i picture in the first box.

1.

2.

3.

4.

5.

6.

7.

Visual Discrimination

Look at each row of pictures. Circle each picture that is the same as the picture in the first box.

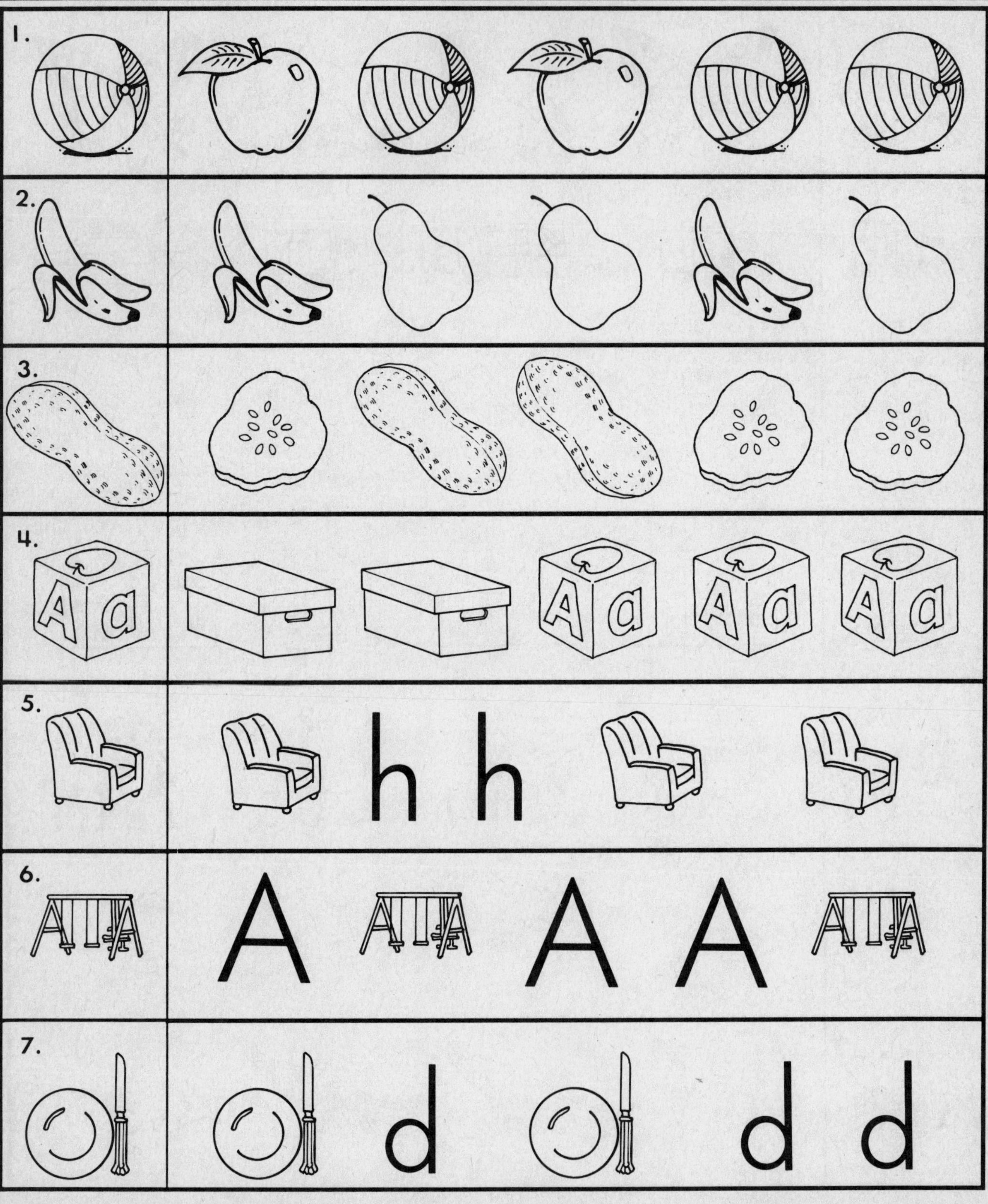

Visual Discrimination

Draw the missing parts in the second picture in each box.

Recognition of Letters: Aa, Bb, Cc

Draw a line to join the matching letters in each box.

1.		2.		3.		4.		5.	
A	A	a	b	B	C	c	c	a	A
B	B	b	a	B	C	b	b	A	a
6.		**7.**		**8.**		**9.**		**10.**	
B	b	C	c	c	a	B	c	C	A
b	B	C	c	a	c	c	B	A	C
11.		**12.**		**13.**		**14.**		**15.**	
B	B	a	B	b	a	c	b	b	b
A	A	B	a	a	b	c	b	c	c

A and a are partner letters. B and b are partner letters. C and c are partner letters. Circle each pair of partner letters. Print each pair of partner letters in the boxes below.

1. Aa	2. Ab	3. Bc
4. Cb	5. Bb	6. Ca
7. Ba	8. Ac	9. Cc
10.	11.	12.

Recognition of Letters: Dd, Ee, Ff

Draw a line to join the matching letters in each box.

1. E D / E D	2. F E / E F	3. D D / F F	4. D d / D d	5. e E / E e
6. F F / f f	7. d e / e d	8. f f / d d	9. e f / e f	10. F E / E F
11. E f / E f	12. E f / f E	13. d d / e e	14. f e / e f	15. d f / d f

D and d are partner letters. E and e are partner letters. F and f are partner letters. Circle each pair of partner letters. Print each pair of partner letters in the boxes below.

1. Dd	2. De	3. Ee
4. Fe	5. Ed	6. Df
7. Ef	8. Ff	9. Fd
10.	11.	12.

Recognition of Letters: Aa, Bb, Cc, Dd, Ee, Ff

Look at the letter in the corner of each box. Circle the same letter each time you see it in the word.

1. d door	2. d spider	3. a ax	4. f fox	5. a zebra
6. c cup	7. e needle	8. b bird	9. d window	10. c tacks
11. b rabbit	12. e eagle	13. a apple	14. f cuff	15. b baby

Look at the letter in the corner of each box. Circle the same letter each time you see it in the words.

1. a acorns came apple band	2. b bell bad baby nibble	3. c cow can crock tack
4. d deer need sled bed	5. e eagle needle eggs see	6. f fill suffer fat feather

Recognition of Letters: Aa, Bb, Cc, Dd, Ee, Ff

Look at the letters in each train car. Draw wheels on the cars that have partner letters. Print the partner letters in each box.

1. Bc Ef Aa

Aa

2. Fb Dd Ce

3. Bb Ed Ac

4. Ca Eb Ff

5. Bc Ee Db

6. Cc De Bd

Recognition of Letters: Gg, Hh, Ii

Draw a line to join the matching letters in each box.

1. H—H / I G	2. I G / I I	3. G G / H G	4. G H / H I	5. I G / G I
6. H I / H I	7. G H / H H	8. H H / G G	9. g i / g i	10. h i / g h
11. i i / h i	12. h g / h g	13. g h / h i	14. i h / h i	15. g g / h h

G and g are partner letters. H and h are partner letters. I and i are partner letters. Circle each pair of partner letters. Print each pair of partner letters in the boxes below.

1. Gg	2. Gi	3. Hi
4. Hg	5. Hh	6. Gh
7. Ih	8. Ig	9. Ii
10.	11.	12.

Recognition of Letters: Jj, Kk, Ll

Look at the letter in the corner of each box. Circle each word that begins with the letter in the corner.

1. J	2. K	3. L	4. j
Dave Jenna Jim John	José Kim Kathy Hallie	Lilia Pedro Larry Ahmed	jam goose jacks joke
5. k	**6. l**	**7. k**	**8. l**
kite key home kitty	bed lamb log lion	kick duck kit keep	leaf leg doll lamp

J and j are partner letters. K and k are partner letters. L and l are partner letters. Circle each pair of partner letters. Print each pair of partner letters in the boxes below.

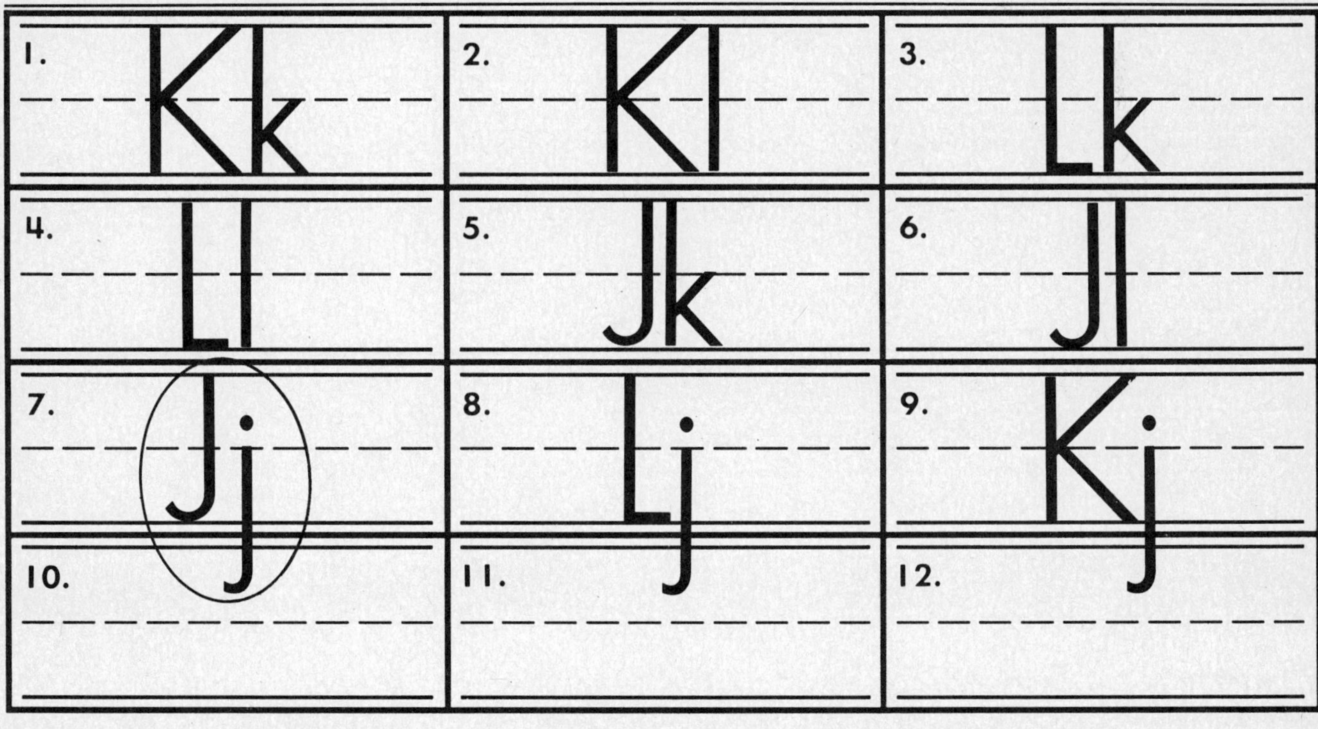

10 Recognition of Letters: All letters from Aa through Ll

Look at the letter in the corner of each box. Circle the same letter each time you see it in the words.

1. g	2. h	3. i
goose wiggle log eggs	hammer much horse father	iron milk inside within

4. j	5. k	6. l
jay jet reject jump	kitten shack rock key	lock fell quilt log

Play Tic-Tac-Toe. Find the three letters in a row that are the same. Draw a line through them. You may find more than one row alike in a game.

1.

i	i	i
j	i	j
j	j	j

2.

h	k	k
k	k	k
h	h	h

3.

b	b	b
b	d	d
d	d	b

4.

c	a	c
a	a	a
c	c	c

5.

f	f	f
f	l	f
l	l	l

6.

j	j	j
g	g	g
g	j	g

7.

e	e	e
e	c	e
c	c	c

8.

b	b	b
b	h	b
h	h	h

9.

i	l	i
i	i	i
l	l	l

10.

d	d	d
b	b	b
d	d	d

Recognition of Letters: All letters from Aa through Ll

Circle the pairs of words that begin with the same letter. Then print the partner letters from Aa through Ll in order in the boxes at the bottom of the page.

1.

crayon
cow

boots	desk	apple
door	deer	can
acorn	baby	cap
ate	bib	cane

2.

fence
fire

horse	house	goat
need	ham	game
eagle	garden	egg
each	quit	cob

3.

kitten
key

lion	kite	ice
lock	hat	jet
lake	is	jam
ice	it	jacks

1. Aa	2.	3.	4.
5.	6.	7.	8.
9.	10.	11.	12.

Recognition of Letters: Mm, Nn, Oo

Look at the letter in the corner of each box. Circle each word that begins with the letter in the corner.

1. M	2. N	3. O	4. m
Nick Mary May March	Nan Manuel Nate Maine	Oz Ohio Rosita Owen	name mane make net
5. n	**6. o**	**7. m**	**8. n**
need mule never mouse	an on ax ox	man milk nest meat	mail nuts nail nice

M and m are partner letters. N and n are partner letters. O and o are partner letters. Circle each pair of partner letters. Print each pair of partner letters in the boxes below.

1. Mn	2. Nm	3. Om
4. No	5. On	6. Mo
7. Mm	8. Nn	9. Oo
10.	11.	12.

Recognition of Letters: Pp, Qq

Draw a line to join the matching letters in each box.

1.	2.	3.	4.	5.
P B / P B	Q O / O Q	Q Q / C C	D P / P D	p P / p P
6.	7.	8.	9.	10.
q q / Q Q	p p / q q	g q / q g	p B / B p	m m / n n
11.	12.	13.	14.	15.
b p / p b	q q / g g	d b / d b	h k / k h	i j / i j

P and p are partner letters. Q and q are partner letters. Circle each word that begins with either partner letter shown in the small box. Print each pair of partner letters in the boxes below.

Recognition of Letters: Mm, Nn, Oo, Pp, Qq

Look at the letter in the corner of each box. Circle the same letter each time you see it in the words.

1. m	2. n	3. o	4. p	5. q
man	nest	oak	pen	quilt
woman	pan	open	pepper	quit
team	nine	dome	drop	begin
simmer	winner	coat	pipe	quart
mow	neat	over	pump	queen
Timmy	banana	foam	apple	guard
worm	nut	close	spider	quiet

Draw leaves on the stems of all apples that show partner letters.

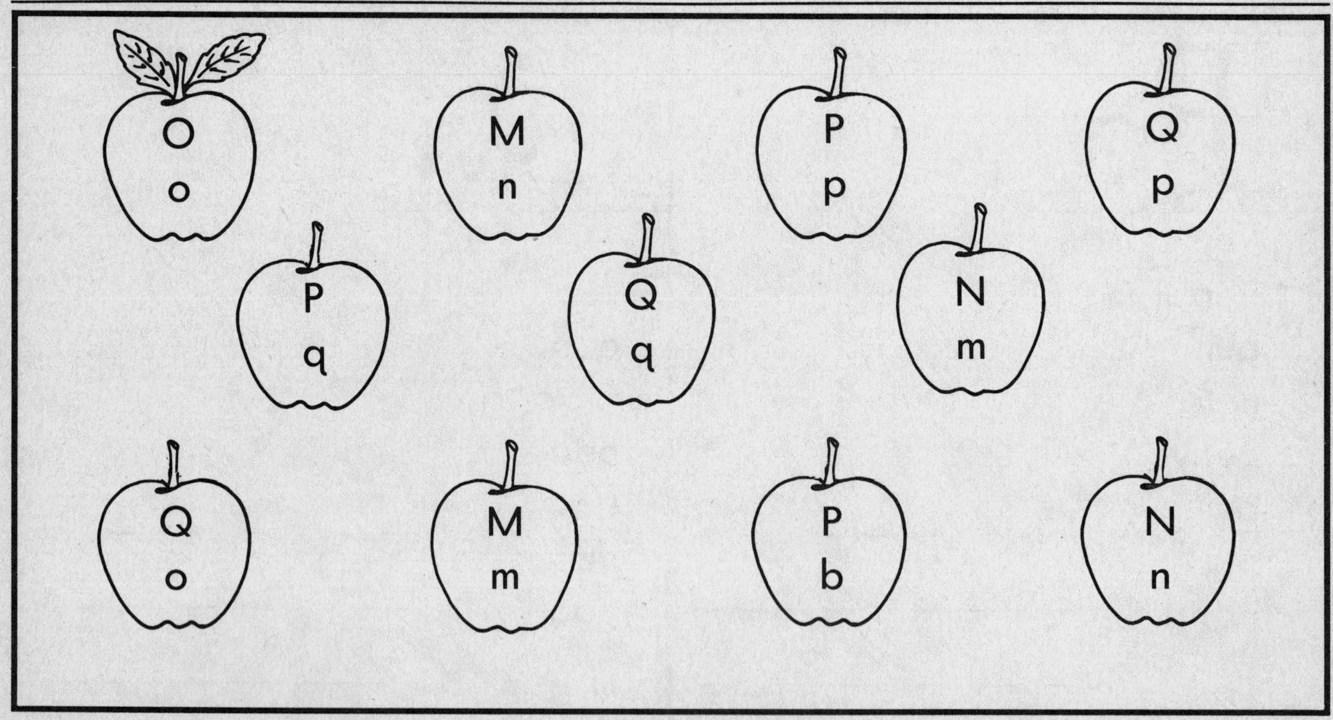

Recognition of Letters: Rr, Ss, Tt

Look at the letter in the corner of each box. Circle each word that begins with the letter in the corner.

1. R	2. S	3. T	4. r
Bob	Sue	Tom	nose
Rose	Queen	Fred	rose
Ross	Sam	Tammy	tire
Pam	Ray	Ted	fire

5. s	6. t	7. r	8. t
scissors	rent	ruler	time
glass	tent	rock	tell
soap	fate	rope	let
six	tomato	near	fat

R and r are partner letters. S and s are partner letters. T and t are partner letters. Circle each pair of partner letters. Print each pair of partner letters in the boxes below.

1. Rs	2. Rr	3. Tr
4. Ss	5. Rt	6. St
7. Ts	8. Sr	9. Tt
10.	11.	12.

Recognition of Letters: Uu, Vv, Ww

Draw a line to join the matching letters in each box.

1.	2.	3.	4.	5.
U V	U U	V W	W V	U W
U V	W W	W V	U V	V U
6.	7.	8.	9.	10.
u u	r u	v v	w v	M W
m n	u s	k r	w m	W N
11.	12.	13.	14.	15.
V N	u u	m w	u u	w v
K V	n m	w v	v v	w v

U and u are partner letters. V and v are partner letters. W and w are partner letters. Circle each pair of partner letters. Print each pair of partner letters in the boxes below.

1. Uu	2. Wv	3. Uw
4. Uv	5. Vv	6. Vw
7. Wu	8. Vu	9. Ww
10.	11.	12.

Recognition of Letters: Xx, Yy, Zz

Draw a line to join the matching letters in each box.

1. X Y / Y X	2. Z Z / X X	3. Y Y / Z Z	4. x y / x y	5. x z / z x
6. y y / z z	7. r n / n r	8. t t / r r	9. i t / i t	10. m n / n m
11. o c / o c	12. i i / l l	13. b d / d b	14. q p / q g	15. t f / f h

X and x are partner letters. Y and y are partner letters. Z and z are partner letters. Circle each pair of partner letters. Print each pair of partner letters in the boxes below.

1. Xx	2. Yx	3. Zy
4. Xz	5. Yy	6. Zx
7. Xy	8. Yz	9. Zz
10.	11.	12.

Recognition of Letters: Letters from Aa through Zz

Look at the letter in the corner of each box. Circle the same letter each time you see it in the words.

1. r	2. s	3. t
rose deer wire read	sat seats visor suits	tent kite tot sit

4. u	5. v	6. w
umbrella fun queen pump	vase weave dive veal	wig weave wick will

7. x	8. y	9. z
ox fox ax x-ray	yarn cry baby yam	zipper size zigzag zoom

Play Tic-Tac-Toe. Find the three letters in a row that are the same and draw a line through them. You may find more than one row alike in a game.

1.

u	u	n
n	n	n
u	u	u

2.

m	m	m
m	r	r
r	r	m

3.

s	z	s
z	z	z
s	s	z

4.

w	w	w
w	v	w
v	v	v

5.

y	x	y
y	y	x
x	x	x

6.

i	i	i
i	l	i
l	l	l

7.

a	e	a
e	e	e
e	a	a

8.

d	d	b
b	d	d
b	b	b

9.

g	g	g
q	q	q
g	q	g

10.

m	n	m
m	m	m
n	n	n

Consonant Sound: S

The word sun begins with the sound of s. Say the name of each picture. If the name begins with the sound of s, print S in the box.

1.  S	2. 	3. 
4. 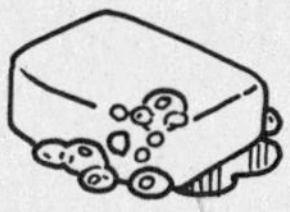	5. 	6. 
7. 	8. 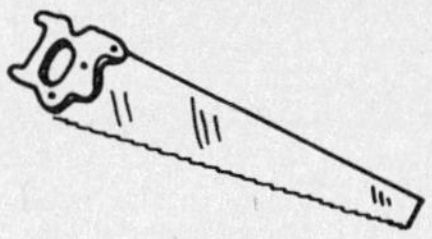	9. 
10. 	11. 	12. 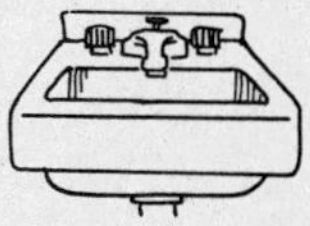

The word dress ends with the sound of s. Say the name of each picture. If the name ends with the sound of s, print s in the box.

1.  s	2. 	3. 
4. 	5. 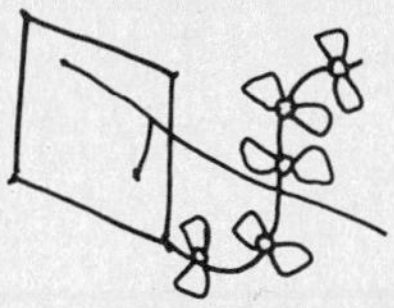	6. 
7. 	8. 	9. 
10. 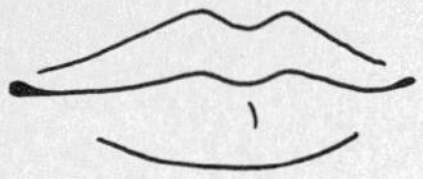	11. 	12. 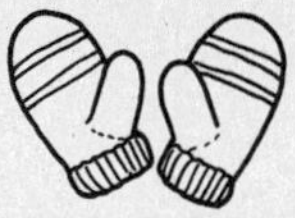

Consonant Sound: T

The word turkey begins with the sound of t. Say the name of each picture. If the name begins with the sound of t, print T in the box.

1. T	2.	3.
4.	5.	6.
7.	8.	9.
10.	11.	12.

The word goat ends with the sound of t. Say the name of each picture. If the name ends with the sound of t, print t in the box.

1. t	2.	3.
4.	5.	6.
7.	8.	9.
10.	11.	12.

Consonant Sounds: S, T

Say the name of each picture. If you hear the sound of s at the beginning of the name, print s in the first box. If you hear the sound of s at the end of the name, print s in the second box.

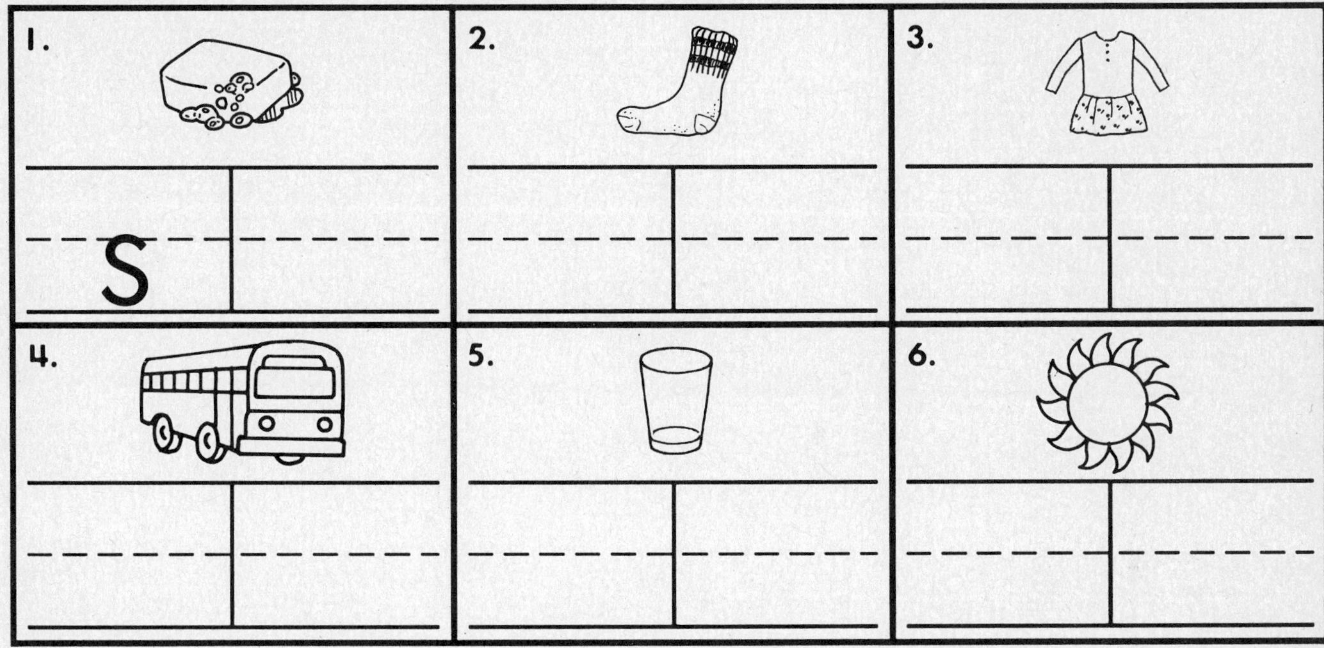

Say the name of each picture. If you hear the sound of t at the beginning of the name, print t in the first box. If you hear the sound of t at the end of the name, print t in the second box.

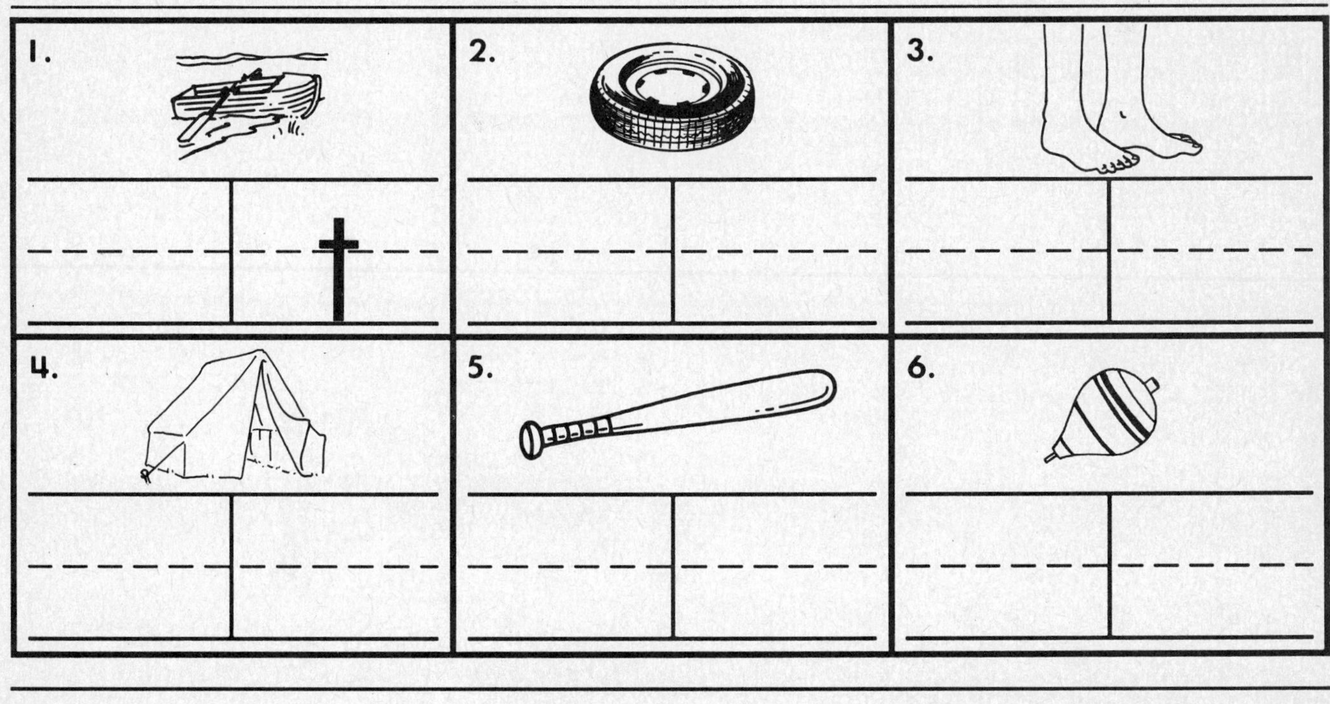

Consonant Sound: B

The word ball begins with the sound of b. Say the name of each picture. If the name begins with the sound of b, print B in the box.

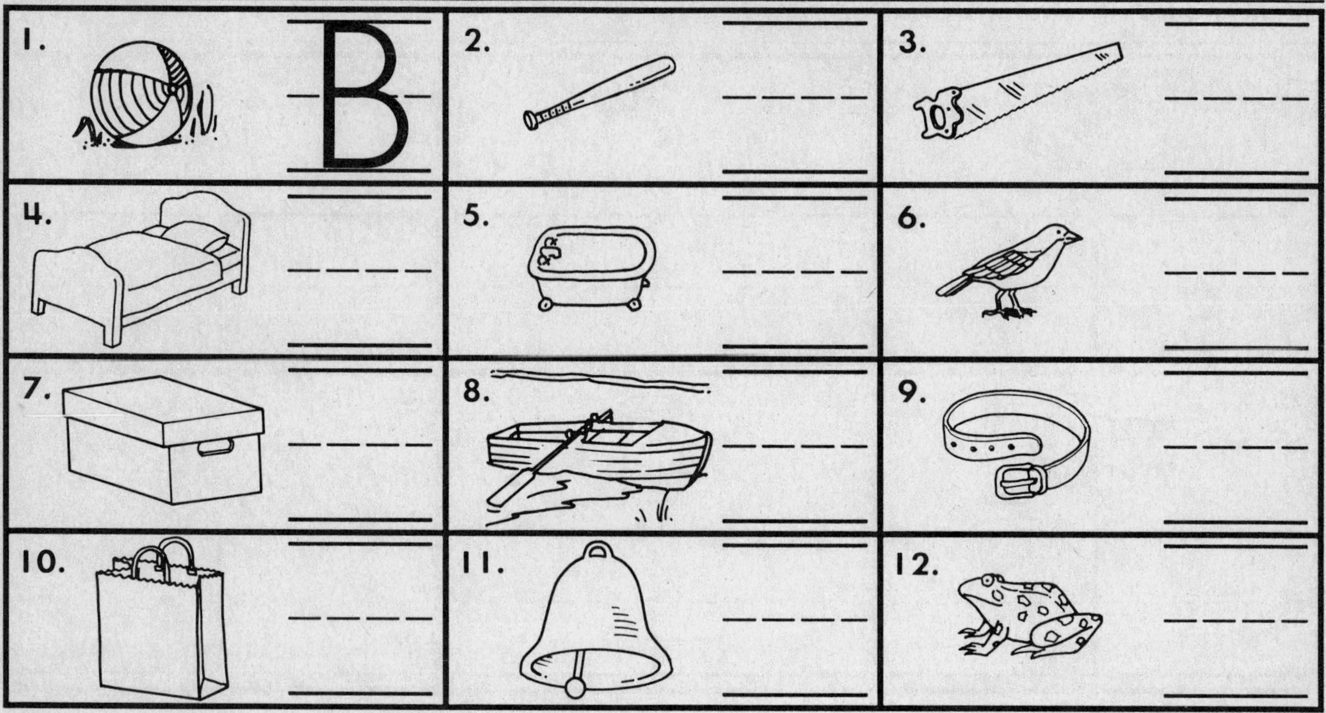

The word web ends with the sound of b. Say the name of each picture. If the name ends with the sound of b, print b in the box.

1. b	2.	3.
4.	5.	6.
7.	8.	9.
10.	11.	12.

Consonant Sounds: B, S, T

Say the name of each picture. If you hear the sound of b at the beginning of the name, print b in the first box. If you hear the sound of b at the end of the name, print b in the second box.

Say the name of each picture. If the name begins with the sound of s, print s in the box. If the name begins with the sound of t, print t in the box.

Consonant Sounds: B, S, T

Say the name of each picture. Circle the beginning letter.

1. s t b 	2. s t b 	3. s t b 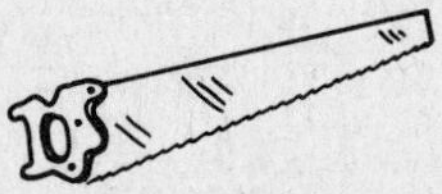
4. s t b 	5. s t b 	6. s t b 
7. s t b 	8. s t b 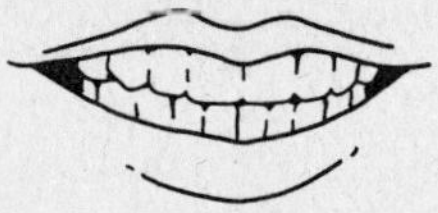	9. s t b 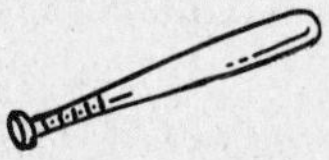
10. s t b 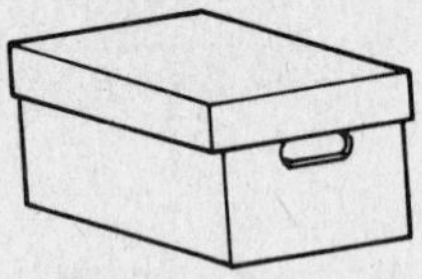	11. s t b 	12. s t b 

Say the name of each picture. If the name begins with the sound of the consonant shown, print the consonant in the first box. If the sound comes at the end, print the consonant in the last box.

1. t 	2. b 	3. t 
4. b 	5. s 	6. b 

Consonant Sounds: B, S, T

Play Tic-Tac-Toe. Draw a line through the three pictures in a row that begin with the same sound. You may find more than one row alike in a game.

1.

2.

3.

4.

Consonant Sound: H

The word hat begins with the sound of h. Say the name of each picture. If the name begins with the sound of h, print H in the box.

1.  H	2. 	3. 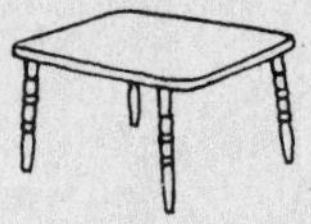
4. 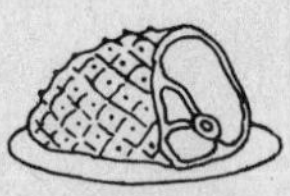	5. 	6. 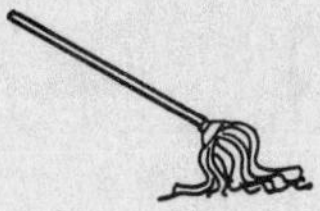
7. 	8. 	9. 
10. 	11. 	12. 

Say the name of each picture. Circle the beginning letter.

1. h s t b 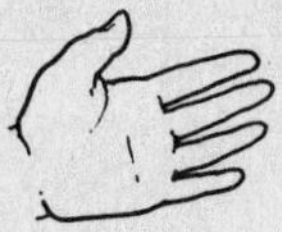	2. h s t b 	3. h s t b 
4. h s t b 	5. h s t b 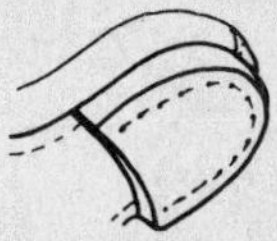	6. h s t b 
7. h s t b 	8. h s t b 	9. h s t b 
10. h s t b 	11. h s t b 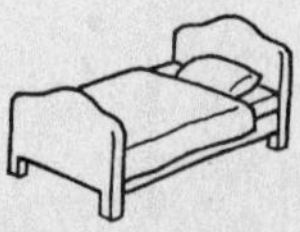	12. h s t b 

Consonant Sound: M

The word moon begins with the sound of m. Say the name of each picture. If the name begins with the sound of M, print m in the box.

1. 	2. 	3. 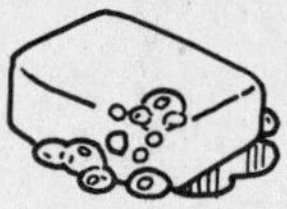
4. 	5. 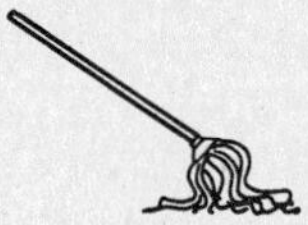	6. 
7. 	8. 	9. 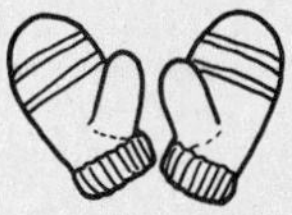
10. 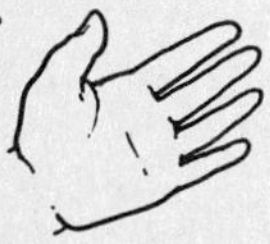	11. 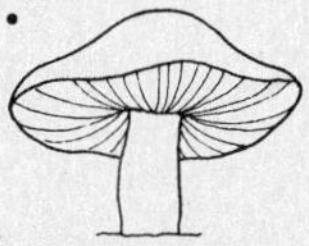	12. 

The word ham ends with the sound of m. Say the name of each picture. If the name ends with the sound of m, print m in the box.

1. 	2. 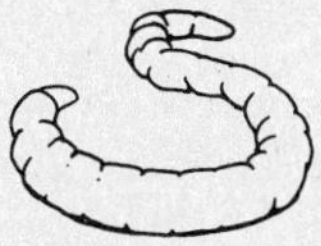	3. 
4. 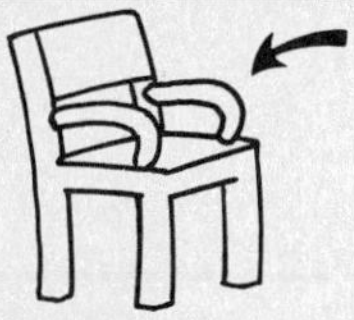	5. 	6. 
7. 	8. 	9. 
10. 	11. 	12. 

Consonant Sounds: B, H, M, S, T

Say the name of each picture. If the name begins with the sound of m, print M in the box. If the name begins with the sound of h, print H in the box.

Say the name of each picture. Print the letters of the beginning and ending sounds in the boxes under the picture.

Consonant Sound: K

The word key begins with the sound of k. Say the name of each picture. If the name begins with the sound of k, print K in the box.

1.  K	2. 	3. 
4. 	5. 	6. 
7. 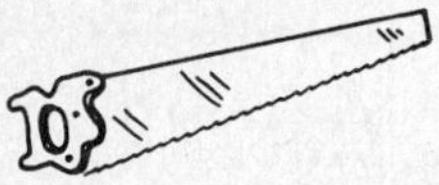	8. 	9. 
10. 	11. 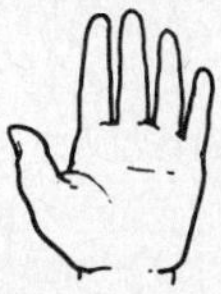	12. 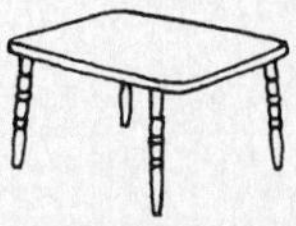

The word truck ends with the sound of k. Say the name of each picture. If the name ends with the sound of k, print k in the box.

1.  k	2. 	3. 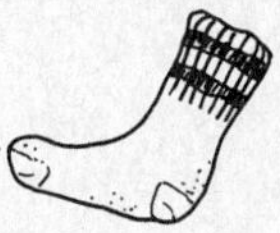
4. 	5. 	6. 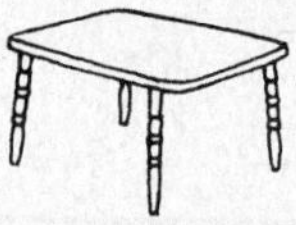
7. 	8. 	9. 
10. 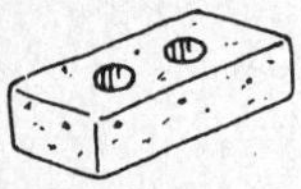	11. 	12. 

Consonant Sounds: H, K, M

Say the name of each picture. If the name begins with the sound of k, print k in the first box. If the name ends with the sound of k, print k in the second box.

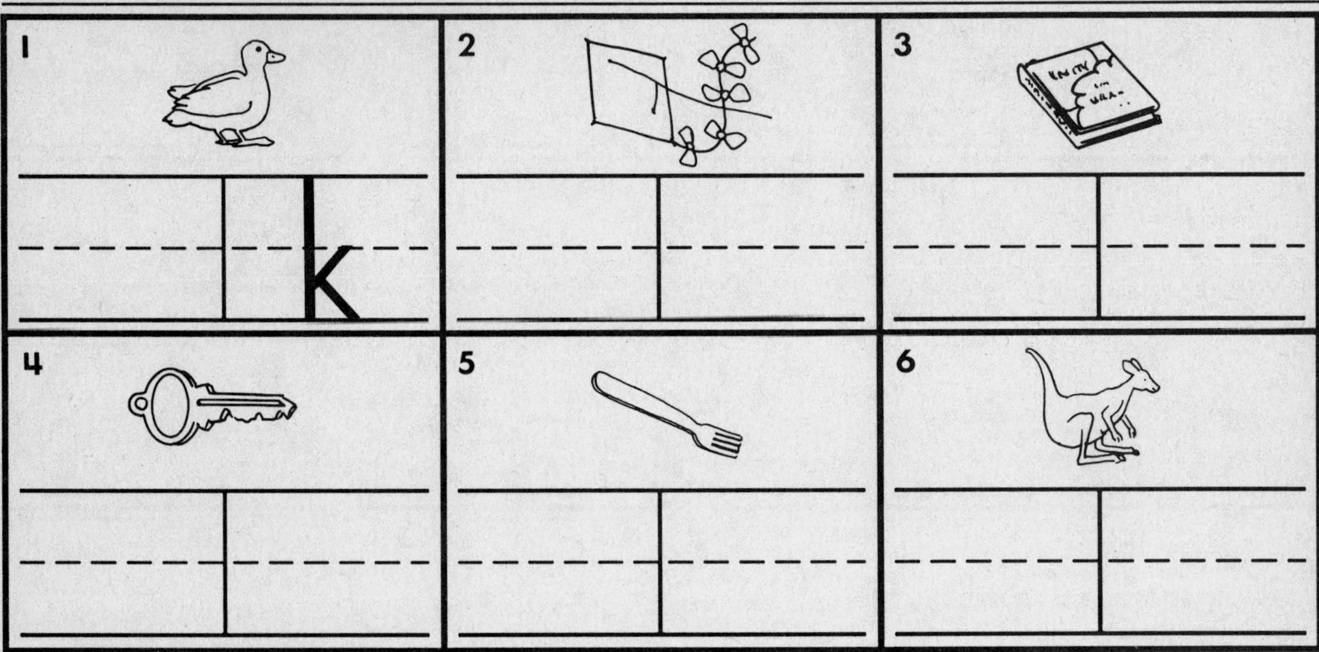

1	2	3
k		
4	5	6

Say the name of each picture. Print the beginning letter in the box.

1. m	2.	3.
4.	5.	6.
7.	8.	9.
10.	11.	12.

Consonant Sounds: B, H, K, M, S, T

Say the name of each picture. Circle the beginning letter.

1. s t b h 	2. s t b h 	3. s t b h 
4. s t b h 	5. s t b h 	6. s t b h 
7. s t b h 	8. s t b h 	9. s t b h 
10. s t b h 	11. s t b h 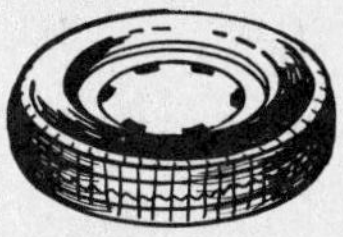	12. s t b h 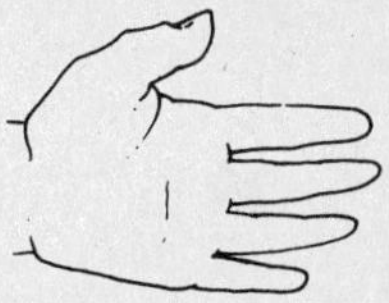

Say the name of each picture. Print the beginning letter in the box.

1. 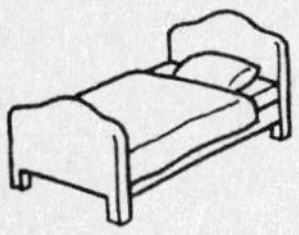 b	2. 	3.  7
4. 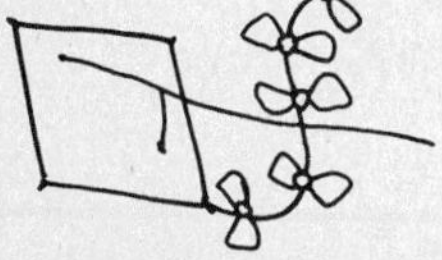	5. 	6. 
7. 	8. 	9. 
10. 	11.  2	12. 

Consonant Sounds: B, H, K, M, S, T

Play Tic-Tac-Toe. Draw a line through the three pictures in a row that begin with the same sound. You may find more than one row alike in a game.

1.

2.

3.

4.

Consonant Sounds: B, H, J, S

The word jet begins with the sound of j. Say the name of each picture. If the name begins with the sound of j, print J in the box.

1.  J	2. 	3. 
4. 	5. 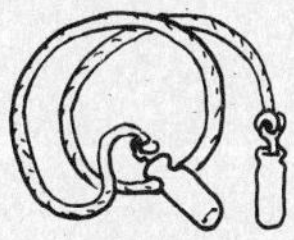	6. 
7. 	8. 	9. 
10. 	11. 	12. 

Say the name of each picture. Circle the beginning letter.

 1. j h (b) s	 2. j h b s	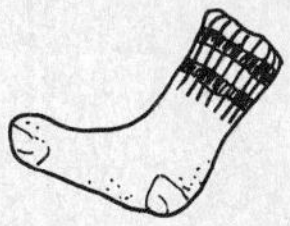 3. j h b s
 4. j h b s	 5. j h b s	 6. j h b s
 7. j h b s	 8. j h b s	 9. j h b s
 10. j h b s	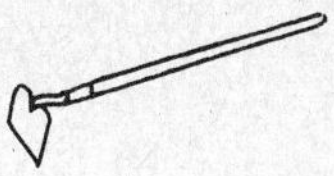 11. j h b s	 12. j h b s

Consonant Sound: F

The word fish begins with the sound of f. Say the name of each picture. If the name begins with the sound of f, print F in the box.

1. F	2.	3.
4.	5.	6.
7.	8.	9.
10.	11.	12.

The word leaf ends with the sound of f. Say the name of each picture. If the name ends with the sound of f, print f in the box.

1. f	2.	3.
4.	5.	6.
7.	8.	9.
10.	11.	12.

Consonant Sounds: B, F, H, J, K, M, S, T

Say the name of each picture. If the name begins with the sound of j, print J in the box. If the name begins with the sound of f, print F in the box.

1. J	2.	3.
4.	5.	6.
7.	8.	9.
10.	11.	12.

Say the name of each picture. Print the letters of the beginning and ending sounds in the boxes under the picture.

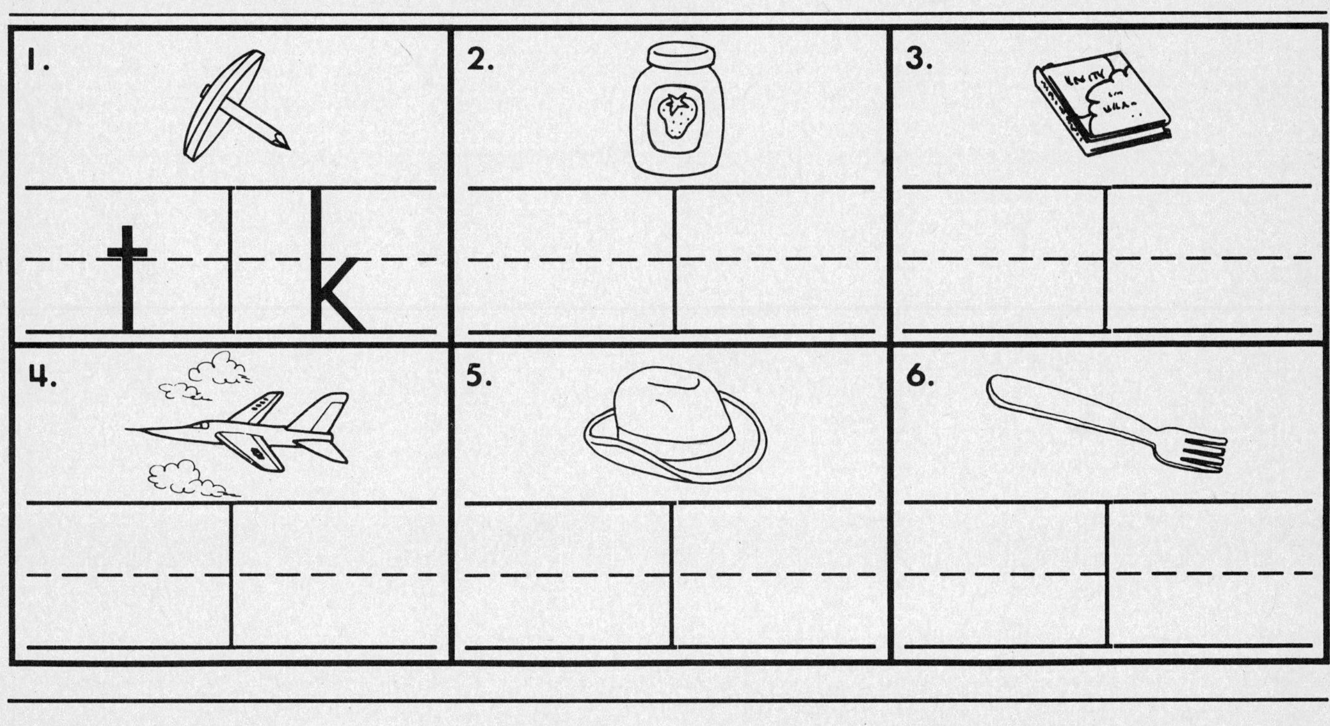

Consonant Sound: G

The word goat begins with the sound of g. Say the name of each picture. If the name begins with the sound of g, print G in the box.

1.  G	2. 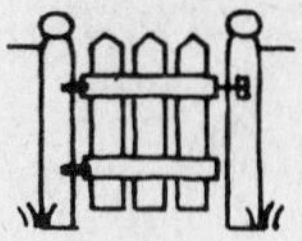	3. 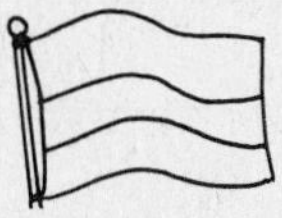
4. 	5. 	6. 
7. 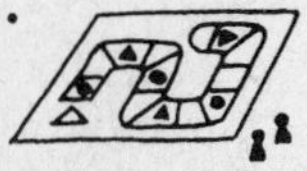	8. 	9. 
10. 	11. 	12. 

The word dog ends with the sound of g. Say the name of each picture. If the name ends with the sound of g, print g in the box.

1.  g	2. 	3. 
4. 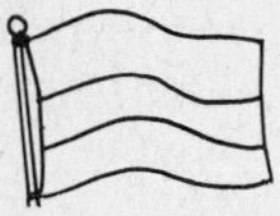	5. 	6. 
7. 	8. 	9. 
10. 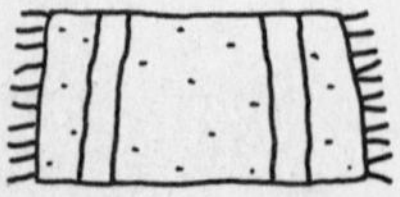	11. 	12. 

Consonant Sounds: B, F, G, H, J, K, M, S,

Say the name of each picture. If the name begins with the sound of g, print g in the first box. If the name ends with the sound of g, print g in the second box.

 1.	2. 	3. 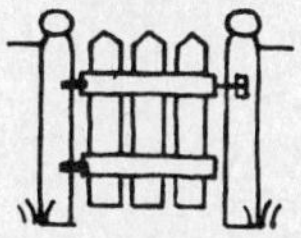
g		
4. 	5. 	6. 

Say the name of each picture. Print the letters of the beginning and ending sounds in the boxes under the picture.

 1.	2. 	3. 
f k		
4. 	5. 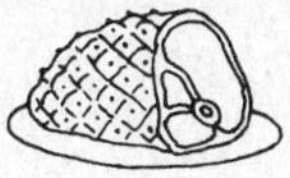	6. 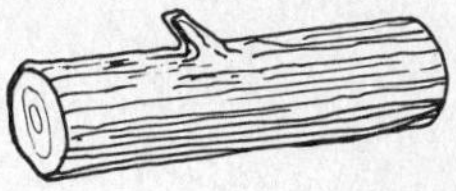

Consonant Sounds: B, F, G, H, J, K, M, S, T

Say the name of each picture. Circle the beginning letter.

1. (j) f g k 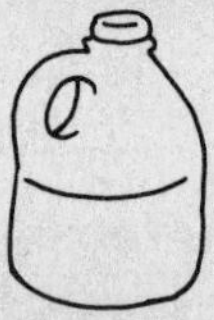	2. j f g k	3. j f g k 
4. j f g k 	5. j f g k 	6. j f g k 
7. j f g k 	8. j f g k 	9. j f g k 
10. j f g k 	11. j f g k 	12. j f g k 

Say the name of each picture. Print the beginning letter in the box.

1. 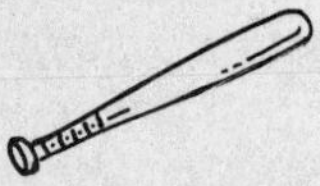 b	2. 	3.
4. 	5. 	6. 
7. 	8.	9. 
10. 	11. 	12. 

Consonant Sounds: B, F, G, H, J, K, M, S, T

Play Tic-Tac-Toe. Draw a line through the three pictures in a row that begin with the same sound. You may find more than one row alike in a game.

1.

2.

3.

4.

Consonant Sound: D

The word dog begins with the sound of d. Say the name of each picture. If the name begins with the sound of d, print D in the box.

1. D	2.	3.
4.	5.	6.
7.	8.	9.
10.	11.	12.

The word toad ends with the sound of d. Say the name of each picture. If the name ends with the sound of d, print d in the box.

1. d	2.	3.
4.	5.	6.
7.	8.	9.
10.	11.	12.

Consonant Sound: L

The word lamp begins with the sound of l. Say the name of each picture. If the name begins with the sound of l, print L in the box.

1. 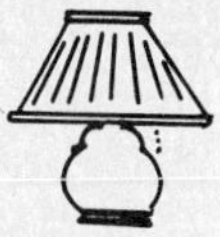 L	2. 	3. 
4. 	5. 	6. 
7. 	8. 	9. 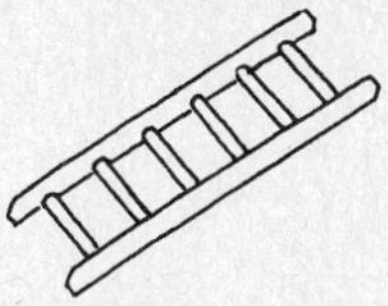
10. 	11. 	12. 

The word bell ends with the sound of l. Say the name of each picture. If the name ends with the sound of l, print l in the box.

1.  l	2. 	3. 
4. 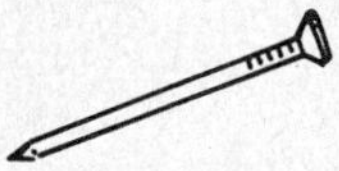	5. 	6. 
7. 	8. 	9. 
10. 	11. 	12. 

Consonant Sounds: D, F, G, J, L, M

Say the name of each picture. Print the beginning letter in the box.

1. l	2.	3.
4.	5.	6.
7.	8.	9.
10.	11.	12.

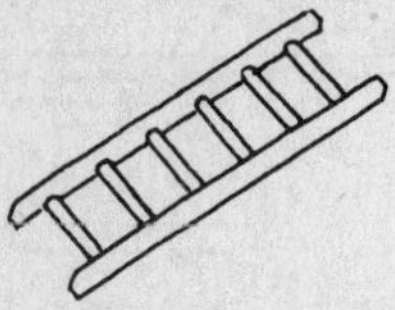

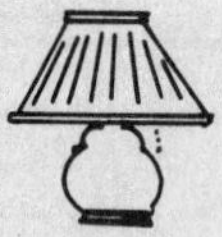

Say the name of each picture. Print the letters of the beginning and ending sounds in the boxes under the picture.

1. l d	2.	3.
4.	5.	6.

Consonant Sound: N

The word nail begins with the sound of n. Say the name of each picture. If the name begins with the sound of n, print N in the box.

1.  N	2. 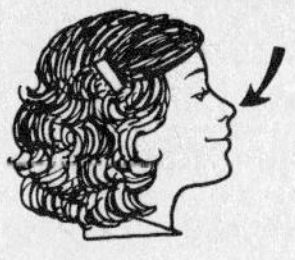	3. 
4. 	5. 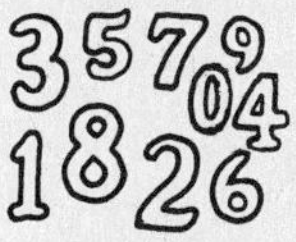 3579 04 1826	6. 
7.	8. 9	9.
10. 	11. 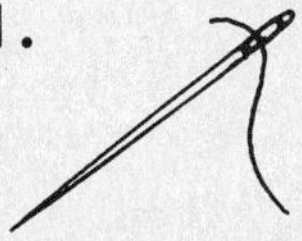	12. 

The word man ends with the sound of n. Say the name of each picture. If the name ends with the sound of n, print n in the box.

1.  n	2. 	3. 
4. 	5.  9	6. 
7. 	8. 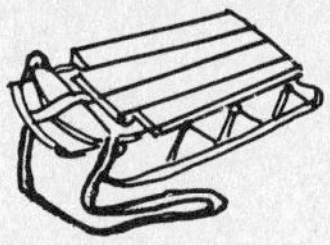	9. 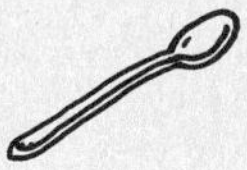
10.	11. 10	12.

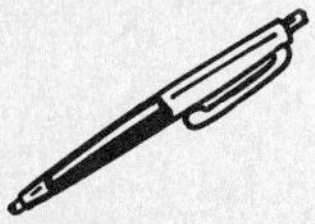

Consonant Sounds: D, F, G, J, L, N

Say the name of each picture. If you hear the sound of n at the beginning of the name, print n in the first box. If you hear the sound of n at the end of the name, print n in the second box.

1. n

2.

3.

4.

5.

6.

Say the name of each picture. Print the letters of the beginning and ending sounds in the boxes under the picture.

1. j g

2.

3.

4.

5.

6.

Consonant Sounds: B, D, F, G, H, J, K, L, M, N, S, T

Say the name of each picture. Circle the beginning and ending letters.

1.  n d m t	2.  j m g l	3. 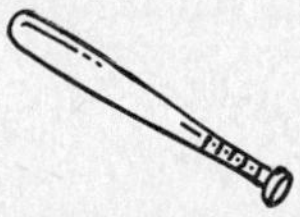 b m d t
4.  j m g n	5.  b k d h	6.  d l b h
7. 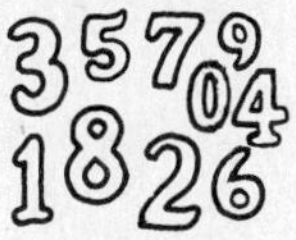 m d n s	8.  t b l f	9.  t m l n
10. 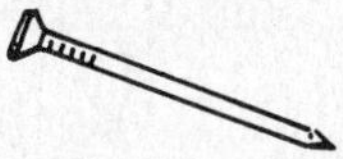 m l n t	11.  f j l g	12.  d l b h

Say the name of each picture. Print the letters of the beginning and ending sounds in the boxes under the picture.

1.  h l	2. 	3. 
4. 	5. 	6. 

Consonant Sounds: D, F, G, H, K, L, M, N, S, T

Play Tic-Tac-Toe. Draw a line through the three pictures in a row that begin with the same sound. You may find more than one row alike in a game.

1.

2.

3.

4.

Consonant Sounds: B, G, L, M, N, W

The word wagon begins with the sound of w. Say the name of each picture. If the name begins with the sound of w, print W in the box.

1. W	2.	3.
4.	5.	6.
7.	8.	9.
10.	11.	12.

Say the name of each picture. Print the letters of the beginning and ending sounds in the boxes under the picture.

1. w m	2.	3.
4.	5.	6.

Consonant Sounds: C, W

The word cat begins with the sound of c. Say the name of each picture. If the name begins with the sound of c, print C in the box.

1.  C	2. 	3. 
4. 	5. 	6. 
7. 	8. 	9. 
10. 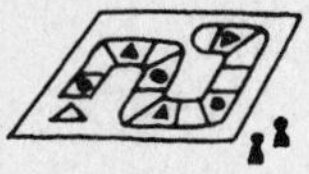	11. 	12. 

Say the name of each picture. Print the beginning letter in the box.

1.  C	2. 	3. 
4. 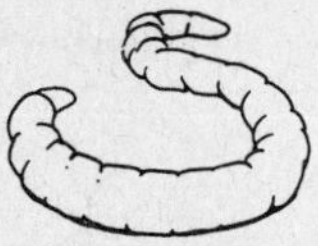	5. 	6. 
7. 	8. 	9. 
10. 	11. 	12. 

Consonant Sounds: C, D, G, L, M, N, W

Say the name of each picture. Circle the beginning and ending letters.

1. s  (w) (l) b	2. h  k n m	3. c  g m n
4. g  c b l	5. w  m c g	6. m  w n m
7. g  c l t	8. h  k t l	9. w 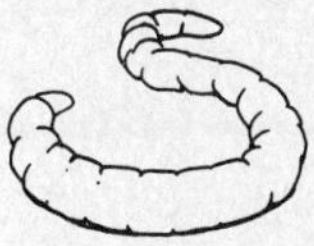 n c m
10. k  h n m	11. m  w b d	12. k  h m n

Say the name of each picture. Print the letters of the beginning and ending sounds in the boxes under the picture.

1. 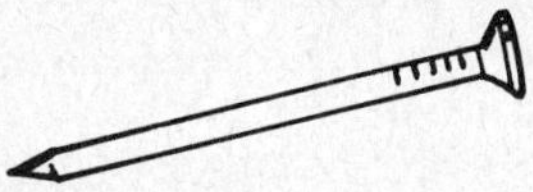 n l	2. 	3. 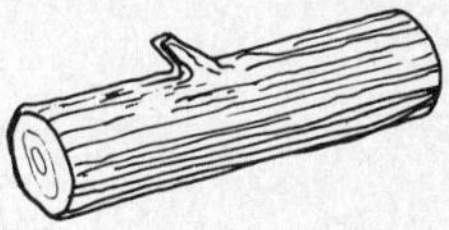
4. 	5. 	6. 

Consonant Sound: R

The word rabbit begins with the sound of r. Say the name of each picture. If the name begins with the sound of r, print R in the box.

1.  R	2. 	3. 
4. 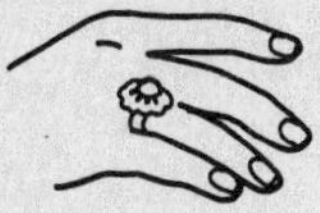	5. 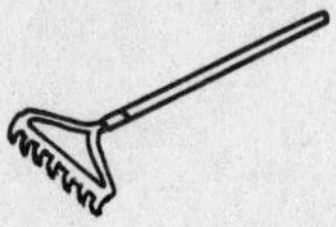	6. 
7. 	8. 	9. 
10. 	11. 	12. 

The word deer ends with the sound of r. Say the name of each picture. If the name ends with the sound of r, print r in the box.

1.  r	2. 	3. 
4. 	5. 	6. 
7. 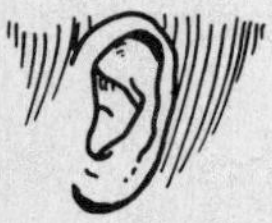	8. 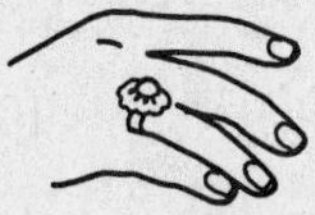	9. 
10. 	11. 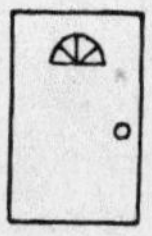	12. 

Consonant Sounds: B, D, L, R, T, W

Say the name of each picture. If you hear the sound of r at the beginning of the word, print r in the first box. If you hear the sound of r at the end of the word, print r in the second box.

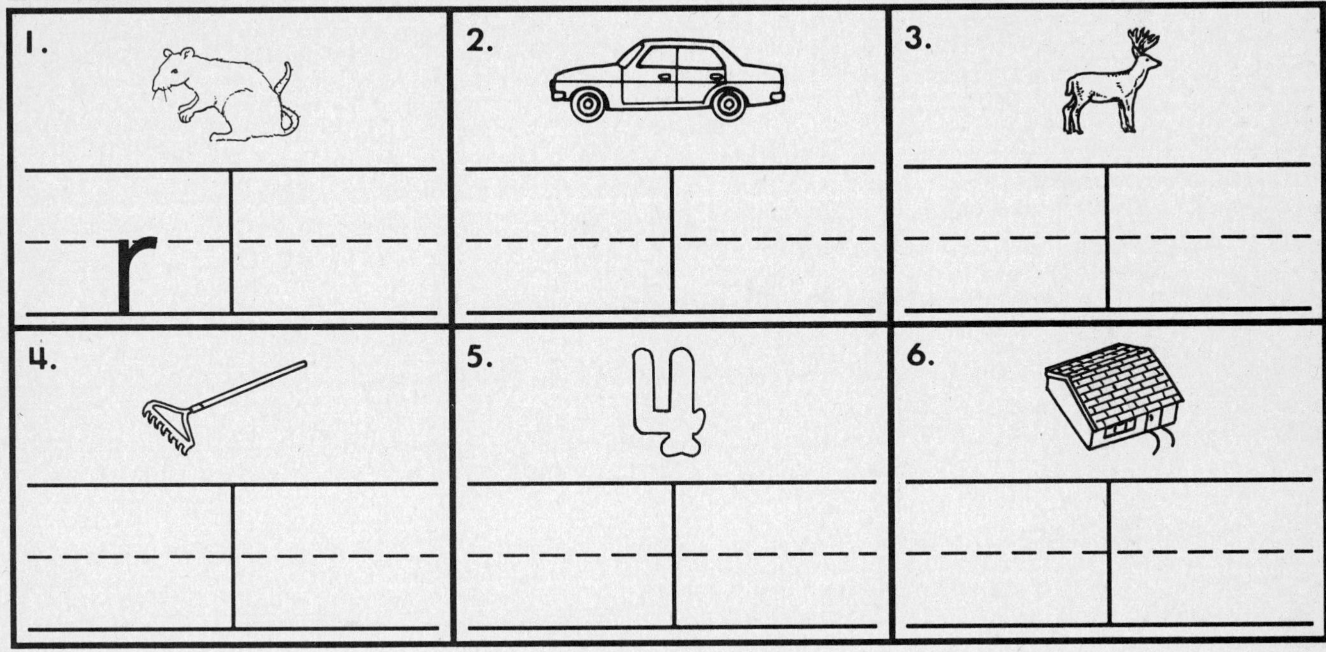

Say the name of each picture. Print the letters of the beginning and ending sounds in the boxes under the picture.

1.	2.	3.
d r		
4.	**5.**	**6.**

Consonant Sounds: C, D, L, N, R, W

Say the name of each picture. Circle the beginning and ending letters.

1. r n  / f b	2. j g  / b r	3. w m  / d b
4. m w  / n m	5. r n  / t l	6. b d  / r s
7. t l  / f m	8. m w  / j g	9. h k  / s n
10. r s  / k h	11. c n 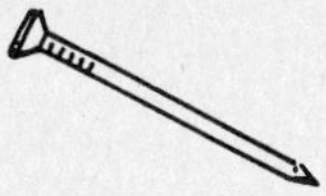 / l g	12. g j  / t d

Say the name of each picture. Print the letters of the beginning and ending sounds in the boxes under the picture.

1.  r d	2. 	3. 
4. 	5. 	6. 

Consonant Sounds: B, C, D, L, N, R, W

Play Tic-Tac-Toe. Draw a line through the three pictures in a row that begin with the same sound. You may find more than one row alike in a game.

1.

2.

3.

4.

Consonant Sound: P

The word pig begins with the sound of p. Say the name of each picture. If the name begins with the sound of p, print P in the box.

1. P	2.	3.
4.	5.	6.
7.	8.	9.
10.	11.	12.

The word cap ends with the sound of p. Say the name of each picture. If the name ends with the sound of p, print p in the box.

1. p	2.	3.
4.	5.	6.
7.	8.	9.
10.	11.	12.

Consonant Sound: V

The word vase begins with the sound of v. Say the name of each picture. If the name begins with the sound of v, print V in the box.

1.  V	2. 	3. 
4. 	5. 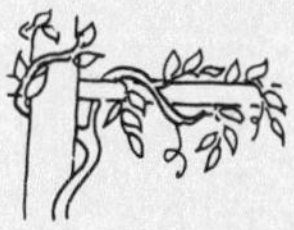	6. 
7. N W E S	8.	9.
10. 	11. 	12. 

The word five ends with the sound of v. Say the name of each picture. If the name ends with the sound of v, print v in the box.

1. 5 v	2.	3.
4. 	5. 	6. 
7. 	8. 	9. 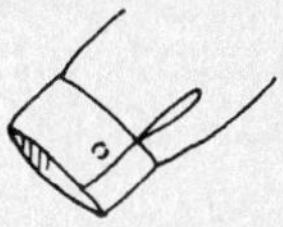
10. 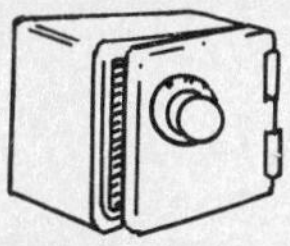	11. 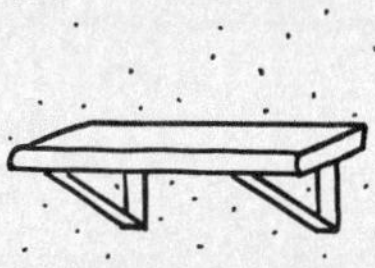	12. 

Consonant Sounds: C, F, L, N, P, R, V, W

Say the name of each picture. Circle the beginning and ending letters.

1.		2.		3.	
w	n	p	t	p	g
v	m	g	m	b	j
4.		**5.**		**6.**	
v	t	n	t	d	r
w	f	r	f	b	n
7.		**8.**		**9.**	
b	t	f	p	c	v
p	l	l	g	r	f
10.		**11.**		**12.**	
w	n	c	f	c	l
v	m	s	v	s	p

Say the name of each picture. Print the letters of the beginning and ending sounds in the boxes under the picture.

1.	2.	3.
v n		
4.	**5.**	**6.**

Consonant Sounds: Qu, X

The word queen begins with the sound of q. Say the name of each picture. If the name begins with the sound of qu, print Qu in the box.

The word box ends with the sound of x. Say the name of each picture. If the name ends with the sound of x, print x in the box.

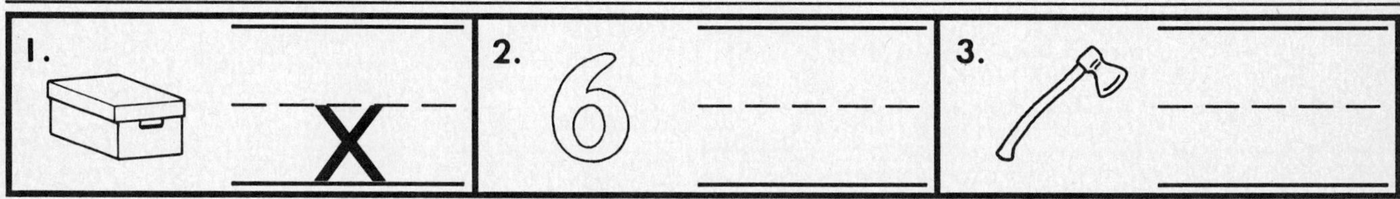

Say the name of each picture. Print the letters of the beginning and ending sounds in the boxes under the picture.

1. qu n

2.

3.

4.

5.

6.

Consonant Sounds: Y, Z

The word yard begins with the sound of y. Say the name of each picture. If the name begins with the sound of y, print Y in the box.

The word zoo begins with the sound of z. Say the name of each picture. If the name begins with the sound of z, print Z in the box.

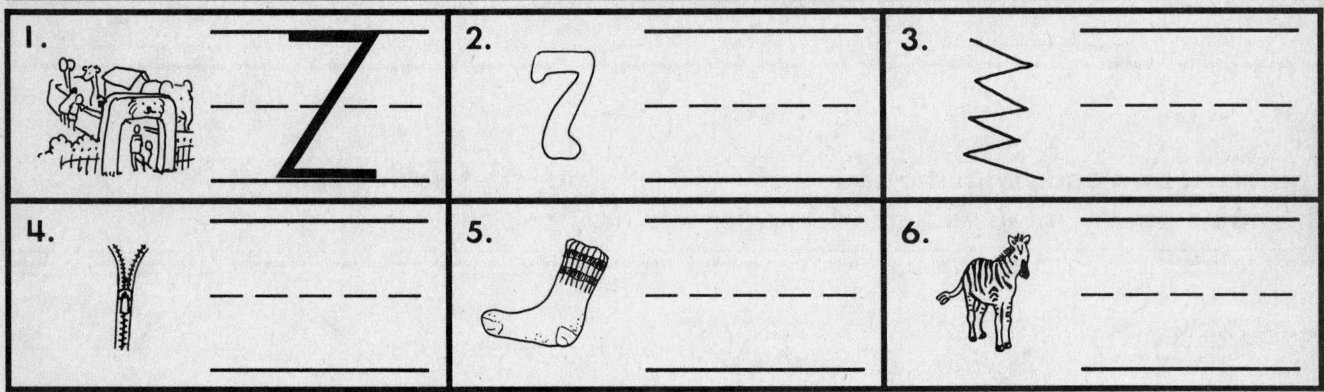

Say the name of each picture. Print the letter of the beginning sound in the box.

1. Z	2.	3.
4.	5.	6.
7.	8.	9.
10.	11.	12.

Consonant Sounds: F, N, P, Qu, R, V, X, Y, Z

Say the name of each picture. Circle the beginning and ending letters.

 1. qu m / g n	 2. w n / v m	 3. z n / s r
 4. y n / x m	 5. qu q / p g	 6. v x / f s
 7. f d / v t	 8. b t / p l	 9. k n / qu m
 10. z n / r m	 11. w d / y s	 12. y m / j n

Say the name of each picture. Print the letters of the beginning and ending sounds in the boxes under the picture.

1.  V t	2. 	3. 
4. 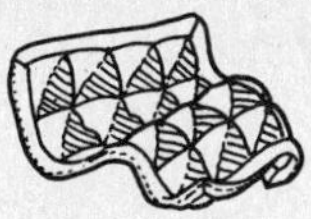	5. 	6. 

Consonant Sounds: K, P, Qu, V, W, X, Y, Z

Play Tic-Tac-Toe. Draw a line through the three pictures in a row that begin with the same sound. You may find more than one row alike in a game.

1.

2.

3.

4.

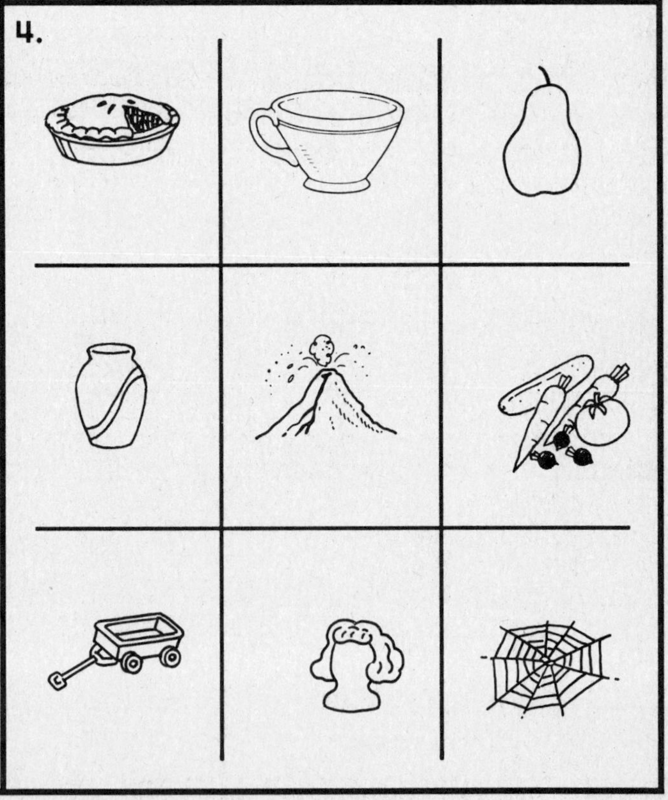

Short Vowel Sound: A

Say the name of each picture. If the name has the short sound of a, print a in the box.

1.  a	2. 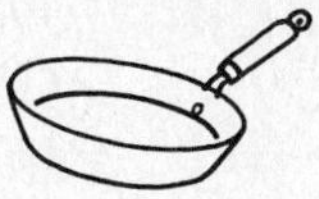	3. 
4. 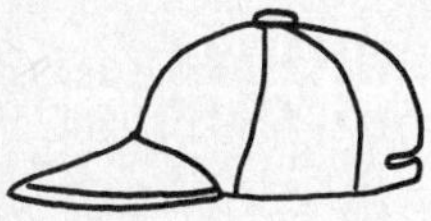	5. 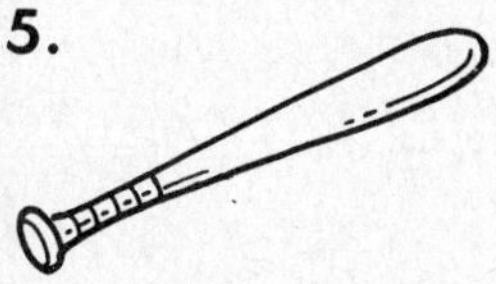	6. 
7. 	8. 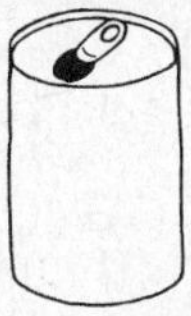	9. 
10. 	11. 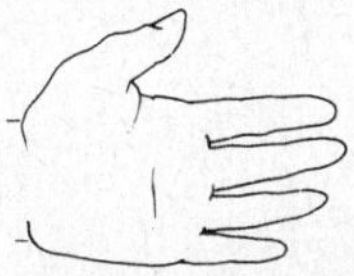	12. 

The word cat has the short sound of a. Say the name of each picture. If the name has the short sound of a, circle the picture.

1. 	2. 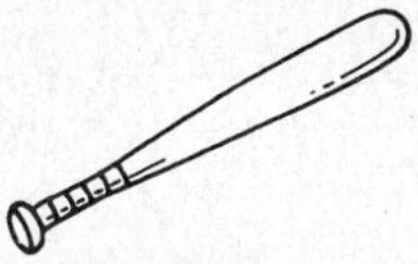	3. 	4. 
5. 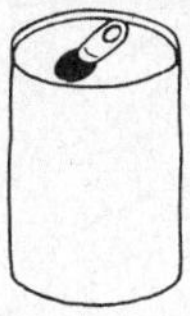	6. 	7. 	8. 
9. 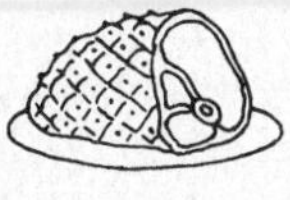	10. 	11. 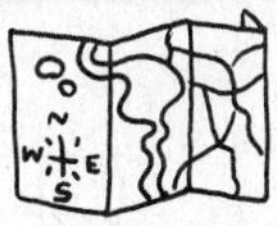	12. 
13. 	14. 	15. 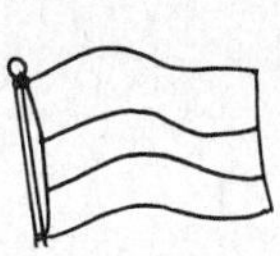	16. 

Short Vowel Sound: A

Say the name of each picture. If the name has the short sound of a, circle the picture.

1. 	2. 	3. 	4. 
5. 	6. 	7. 	8. 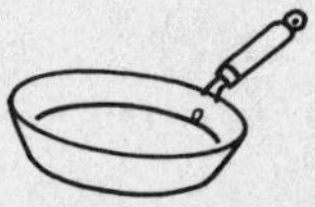
9. 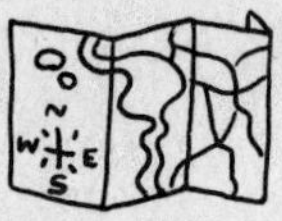	10. 	11. 	12. 
13. 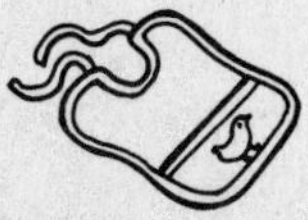	14. 	15. 	16. 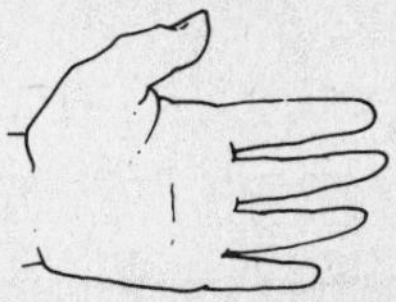

Say the name of each picture. Circle its name.

1.  fat cat mat	2.  jam dam ham	3.  fat fan ran
4.  rat ran bat	5.  bag rag tag	6.  ham dam ram
7.  tan ax tax	8.  jam ran man	9. 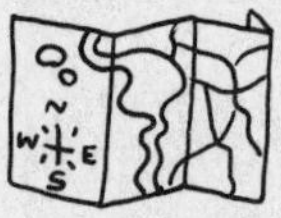 man nap map
10.  ran fan can	11.  rat ran sat	12.  tag sag rag

Short Vowel Sound: A

Say the name of each picture. Circle its name.

1. hat ham rat bat	2. cat man van can
3. dab tab cat cab	4. bag tag rag tap
5. rat man mat cat	6. bag bad bat gab
7. can pan fan pat	8. jam ham dam jab
9. jacks tags sacks tacks	10. at and tax ax

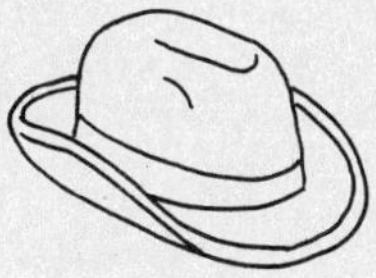

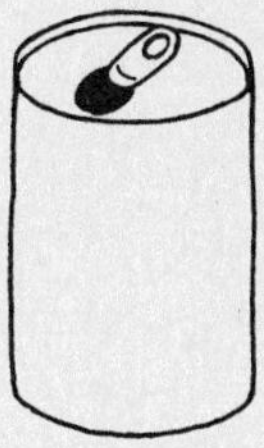

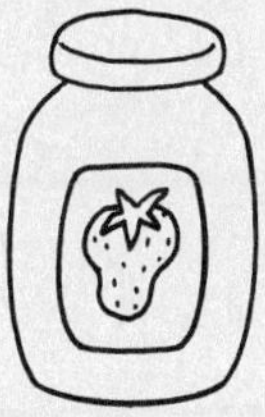

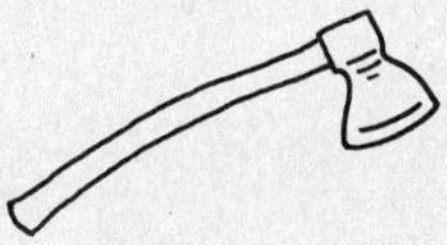

Short Vowel Sound: A

Say the name of each picture. Print the ending consonant of its name in the box.

Say the name of each picture. Print the beginning and ending consonants of its name in the box.

1. man	2. a
3. a	4. a
5. $4.59 a	6. a
7. a	8. a

Short Vowel Sound: A

Look at the picture. Circle the word that will finish the sentence. The word you pick will be the name of the picture. Print the word in the box.

1. Pam has a fat rat.	bat (rat) hat
2. The man has a ________.	ham bat hat
3. Jan has an ________.	wax ax tax
4. Jack has a ________.	bat jam ham
5. Pam can pass the ________.	tack jam mat
6. The man can pack the ________.	bag tag bat
7. The cat ran past the ________.	fan fat pan
8. The ________ had a nap.	cab rat cat

Short Vowel Sound: A

Say the name of each picture. Print its name in the box.

1. fan	2.
3.	4.
5.	6.
7.	8.
9.	10.
11.	12.
13.	14.
15.	16.
17.	18.

Short Vowel Sound: A

Read the words that are part of each sentence. Finish the sentence by writing the words from the box in the correct order.

1. Pam had a cap.	a cap had
2. The fat cat ______.	a has pal
3. Sam can ______.	the bag pack
4. Jan has ______.	fat a ham
5. The fat ______.	fast ran rat
6. Ann can ______.	pass pan the
7. The man ______.	hat a has
8. Jack ______.	tag can Dan

Short Vowel Sound: I

Say the name of each picture. If the name has the short sound of i, print i in the box.

1.  i	2. 	3. 
4. 	5. 	6. 
7. 	8. 	9. 
10. 	11. 	12. 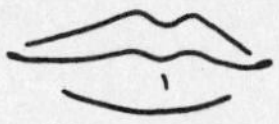

The word pig has the short sound of i. Say the name of each picture. If the name has the short sound of i, circle the picture.

1. 	2. 	3. 	4. 
5. 	6. 	7. 	8. 
9. 	10. 	11. 	12. 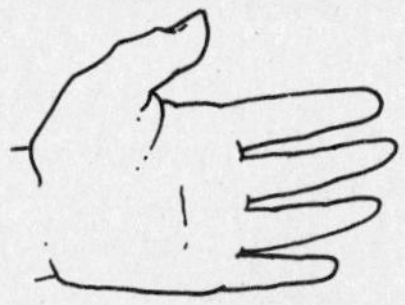
13. 	14. 	15. 	16. 

Short Vowel Sound: I

Say the name of each picture. If the name has the short sound of i, circle the picture.

1. 	2. 	3. 	4. 
5. 	6. 	7. 	8. 
9. 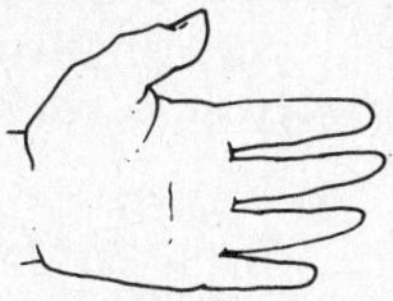	10. 	11. 	12. 
13. 	14. 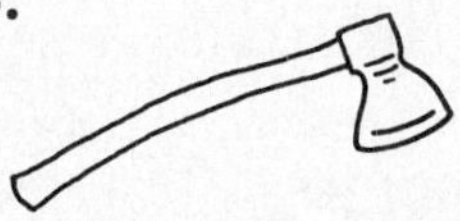	15. 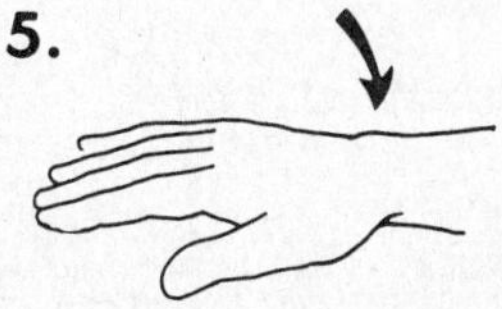	16. 

Say the name of each picture. Circle its name.

1.  rig big pig	2.  win pin tin	3.  pan pin pig
4.  rid lid lad	5.  six fix mix	6. 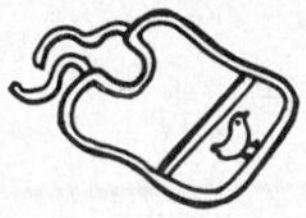 bit bin bib
7.  hill Bill him	8.  mat mitt mill	9. 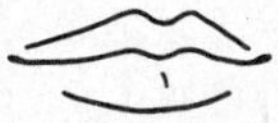 lips laps lisp
10.  lips rim slip	11. 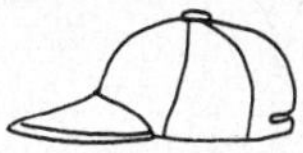 cat cap can	12.  silk milk mill

Short Vowel Sound: I

Say the name of each picture. Circle its name.

1. bib big bid bit	2. hid lid did lit
3. big fig pig pick	4. win big wick wig
5. fix mix wax six	6. tin fin pin pit
7. fill pill hill hit	8. mitt sit fit mill
9. sack tack silk sick	10. lids lips laps lisp

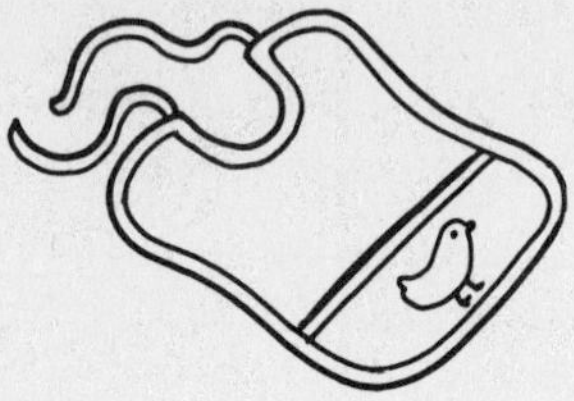

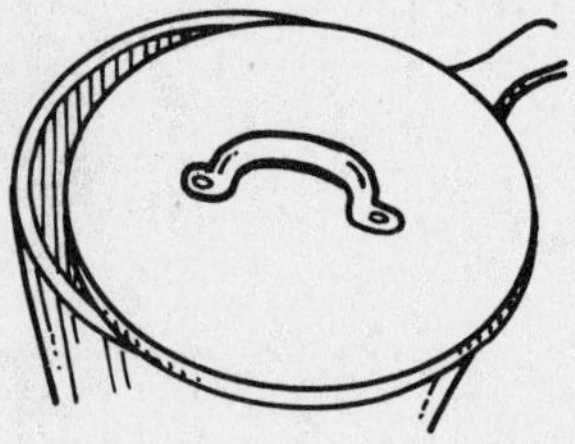

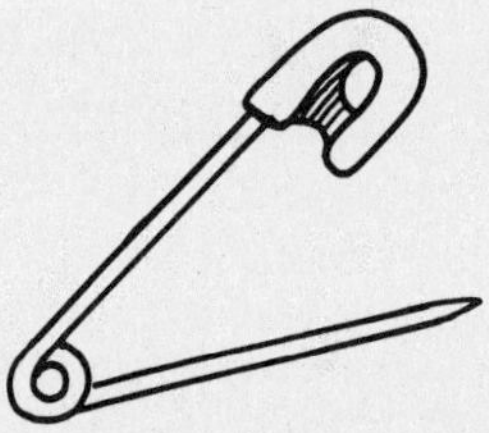

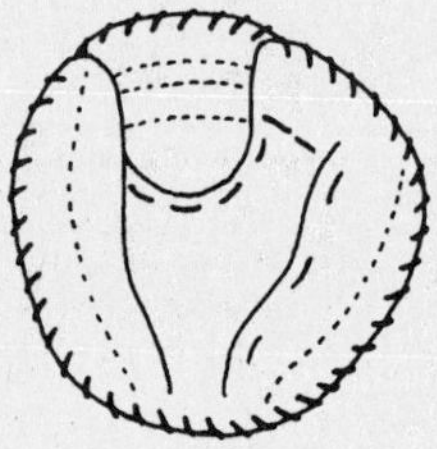

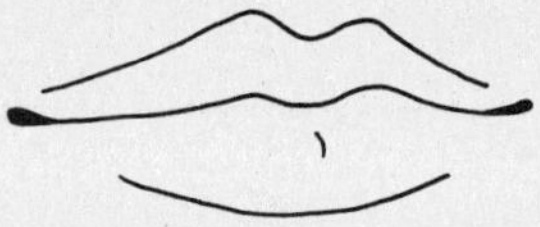

Short Vowel Sound: I

Say the name of each picture. Print the ending consonant of its name in the box.

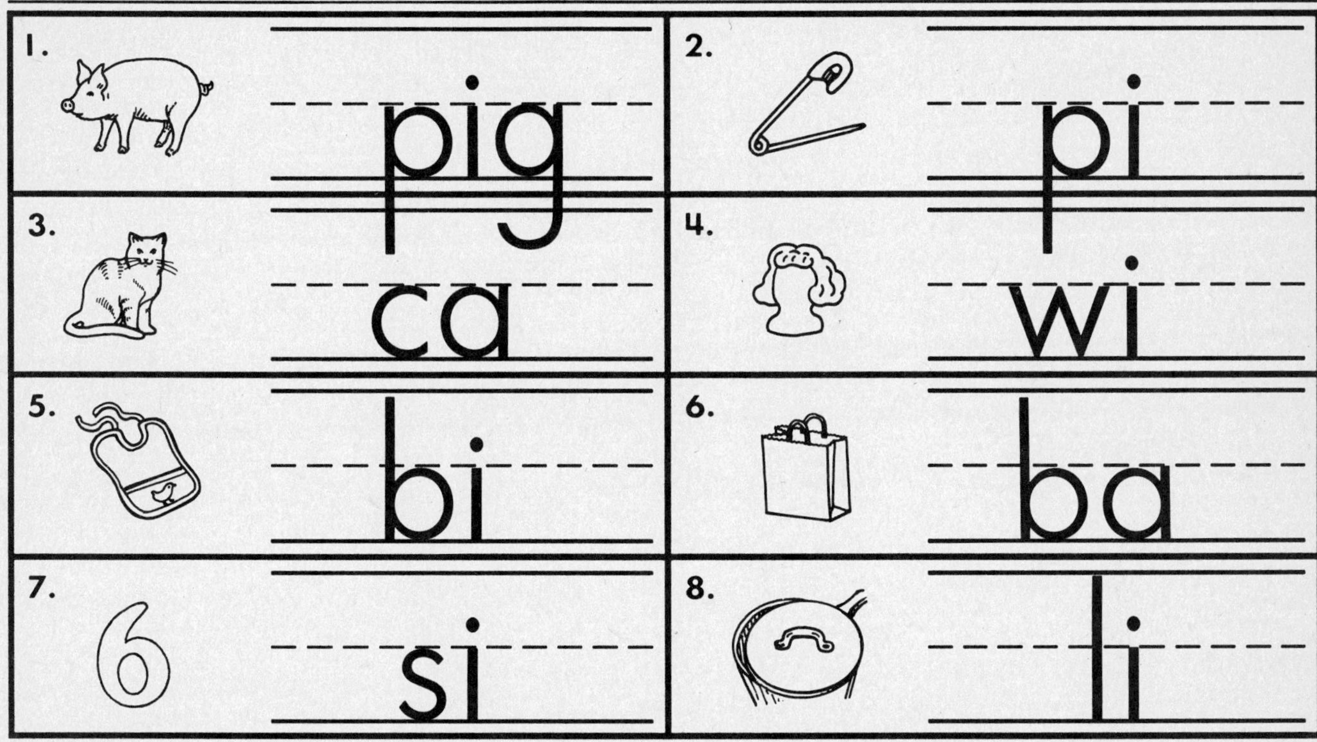

Say the name of each picture. Print the beginning and ending consonants of its name in the box.

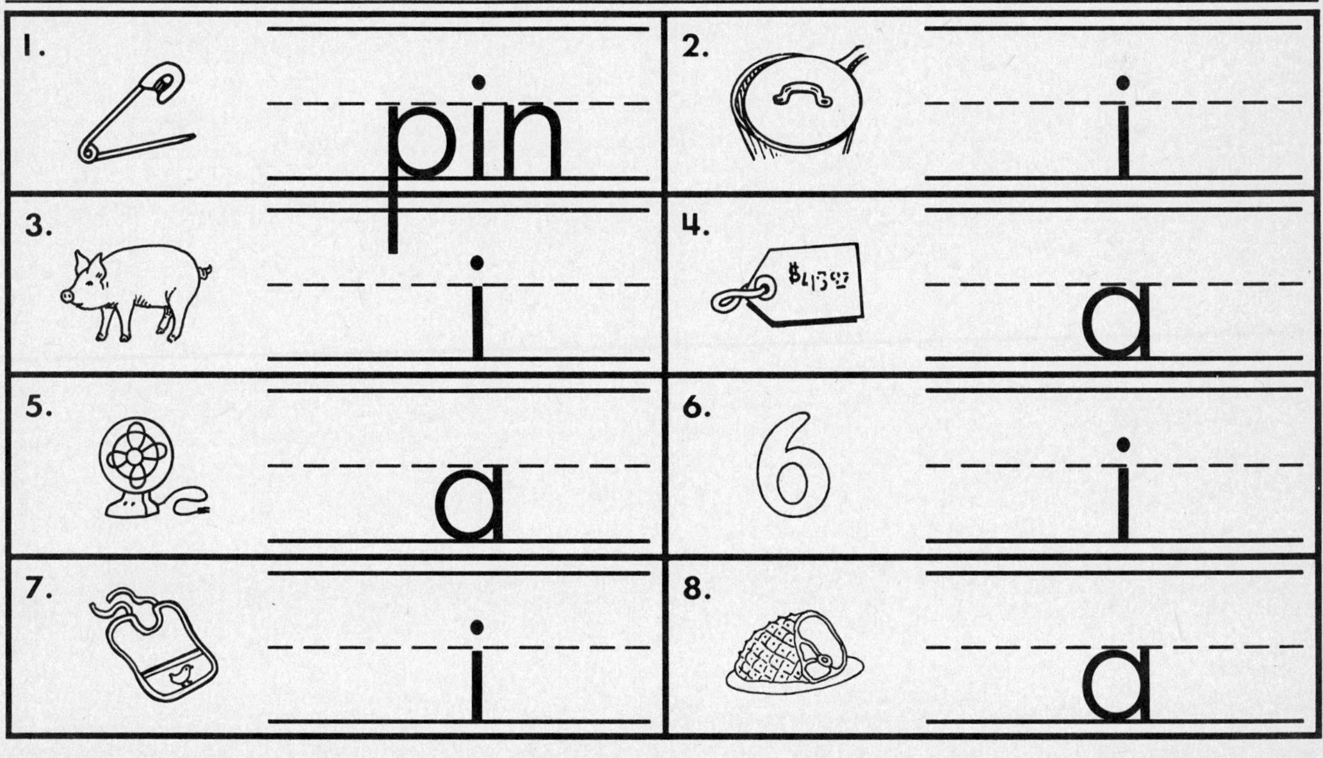

Short Vowel Sound: I

Look at the picture. Circle the word that will finish the sentence. The word you pick will be the name of the picture. Print the word in the box.

1.	Jill will pin the bib.	bid (bib) rib
2.	Ann has a big ________.	wig rig wit
3.	Bill hid the ________.	bat had hat
4.	The man had a sick ________.	big pig pin
5.	The ________ is big and fat.	rat rag cat
6.	The ________ will fit the pan.	hid lid lad
7.	The ________ is in the bib.	pin pan pit
8.	Jim will hit the tin ________.	ran can cap

Short Vowel Sound: I

Say the name of each picture. Print its name in the box.

1. hill	2.
3.	4. 6
5.	6.
7.	8.
9.	10.
11.	12.
13.	14.
15.	16.
17.	18.

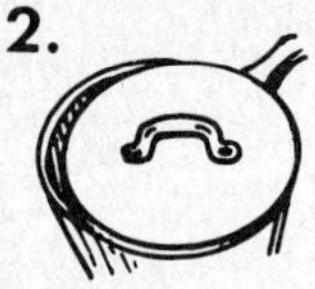

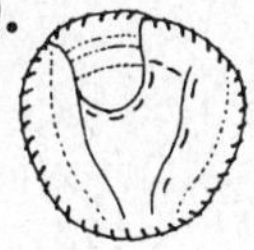

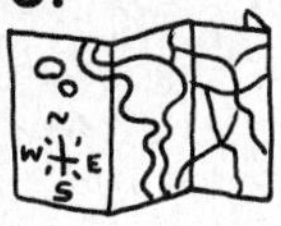

Short Vowel Sound: I

Read the words that are part of a sentence. Finish the sentence by writing the words from the box in the correct order.

1. The can is in the bag.	bag the in
2. The fat cat ______.	the wig hid
3. Kit will dig ______.	in sand the
4. Jan has a ______.	ham big fat
5. Bill will ______.	the bat fix
6. The cat can ______.	the rip sack
7. The man will ______.	six quit at
8. The lid will fit ______.	pan big the

Short Vowel Sound: U

Say the name of each picture. If the name has the short sound of u, print u in the box.

1.  u	2. 	3. 
4. 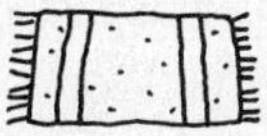	5. 	6. 
7. 	8. 	9. 
10. 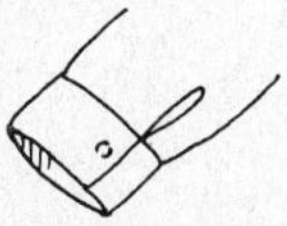	11. 	12. 

The word sun has the short sound of u. Say the name of each picture. If the name has the short sound of u, circle the picture.

1. 	2. 	3. 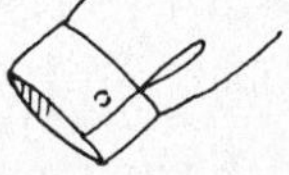	4. 
5. 	6. 	7. 	8. 
9. 	10. 	11. 	12. 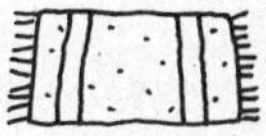
13. 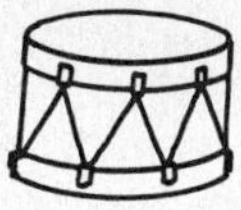	14. 	15. 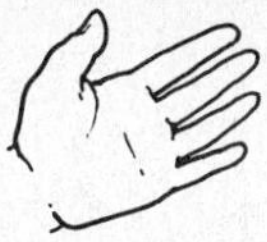	16. 

Short Vowel Sound: U

Say the name of each picture. If the name has the short sound of u, circle the picture.

1.	2.	3.	4.
5.	6.	7.	8.
9.	10.	11.	12.
13.	14.	15.	16.

Say the name of each picture. Circle its name.

 1. cup pup cub	 2. cut sat cat	 3. but dug bug
 4. Dick duck luck	 5. wig wag win	 6. run fun sun
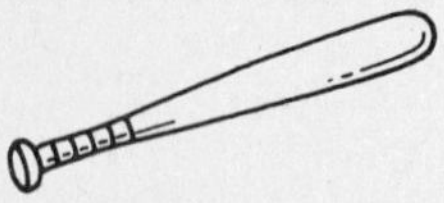 7. bat but bit	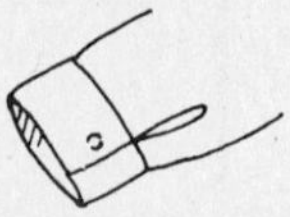 8. cab calf cuff	 9. rub tub tug
 10. dim drum hum	 11. cup pug pup	 12. pig big pin

Short Vowel Sound: U

Say the name of each picture. Circle its name.

1. bug but bag big	2. bat but tub tab
3. Dick duck back buck	4. suck silk mill milk
5. cap cup cuff cub	6. bud bad bid but
7. jog hug jug lug	8. bucks ducks backs tacks
9. sun run six ran	10. cuff muff cub milk

Short Vowel Sound: U

Say the name of each picture. Print the ending consonant of its name in the box.

Say the name of each picture. Print the beginning and ending consonants of its name in the box.

1. bus	2. u
3. u	4. a
5. u	6. u
7. i	8. u

Short Vowel Sound: U

Look at the picture. Circle the word that will finish the sentence. The word you pick will be the name of the picture. Print the word in the box.

1.	Bill will fill the ______.	cup (circled) cap pup
2.	Jill ran up the ______.	pill hill sill
3.	Ann sat in the ______.	bus bun hum
4.	Sam will fix the ______.	pan fun fan
5.	Dick has a ______.	pan pup cup
6.	Pat has a bug in the tin ______.	fan cub can
7.	The cub sat in the ______.	sun run sum
8.	The ______ is on the rug.	big hug bug

Short Vowel Sound: U

Say the name of each picture. Print its name in the box.

1. bus	2.
3.	4.
5.	6.
7.	8.
9.	10.
11.	12.
13.	14.
15.	16.
17.	18.

Short Vowel Sound: U

Read the words that are part of a sentence. Finish the sentence by writing the words from the box in the correct order.

1. Jack and Jill ran up the hill .	the hill up
2. The tub is __________ .	full mud of
3. The bug is in __________ .	tin the cup
4. The big pan is __________ .	sand full of
5. Ann hid the cat __________ .	tub in the
6. A bug in the __________ .	bit bus Gus
7. Pat has a pup __________ .	in hands his
8. The big man sat __________ .	bus in the

Short Vowel Sound: O

Say the name of each picture. If the name has the short sound of o, print o in the box.

1.  O	2. 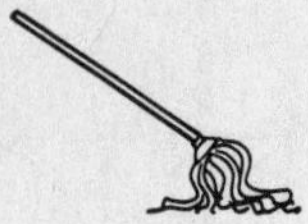	3. 
4. 	5. 	6. 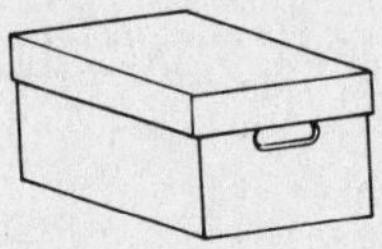
7. 	8. 	9. 
10. 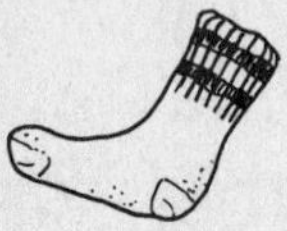	11. 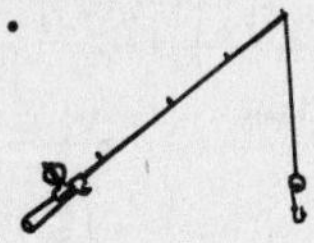	12. 

The word fox has the short sound of o. Say the name of each picture. If the name has the short sound of o, circle the picture.

1. 	2. 	3. 	4. 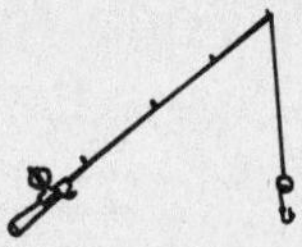
5. 	6. 	7. 	8. 
9. 	10. 	11. 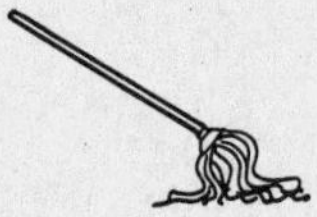	12. 
13. 	14. 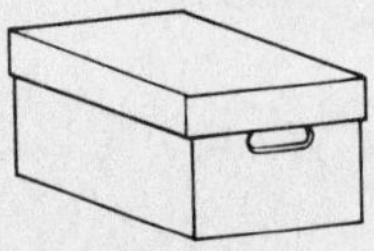	15. 	16. 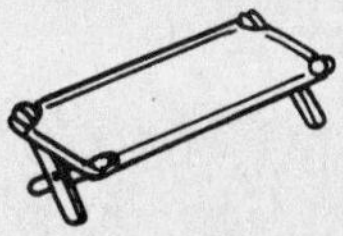

Short Vowel Sound: O

Say the name of each picture. If the name has the short sound of o, circle the picture.

1. 	2. 	3. 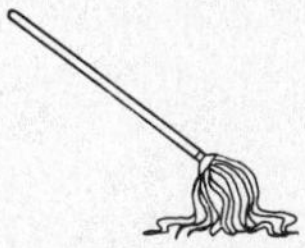	4. 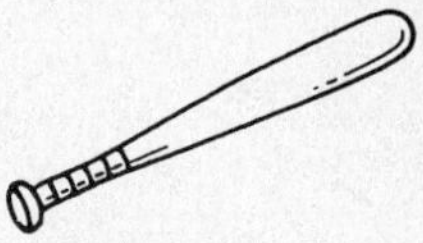
5. 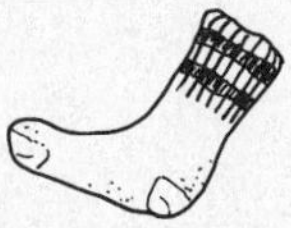	6. 	7. 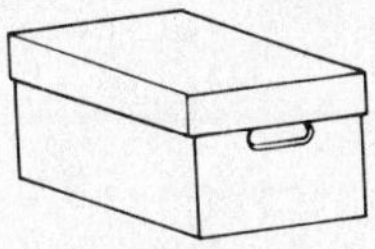	8. 
9. 	10. 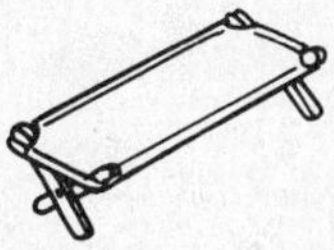	11. 	12. 
13. 	14. 	15. 	16. 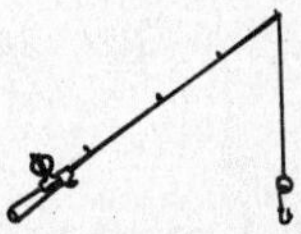

Say the name of each picture. Circle its name.

1. 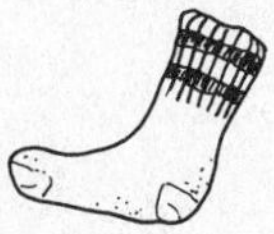 sick sack sock	2.  lock luck lack	3.  tip tap top
4. 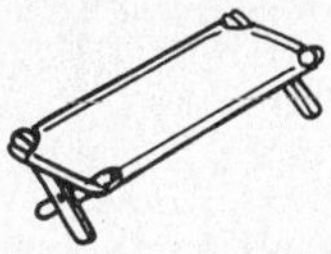 cot cut cap	5. 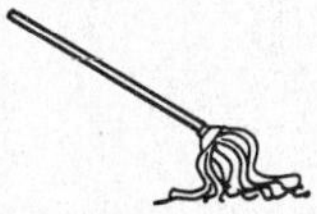 map mat mop	6.  sack sock suck
7.  coat cat cape	8.  bug pig pin	9.  nut not nod
10.  pit pat pot	11.  rack run rock	12. 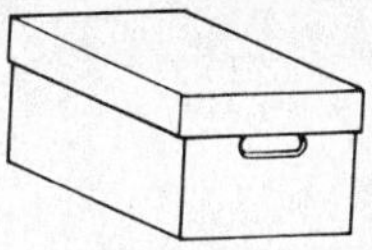 box bat but

Short Vowel Sound: O

Say the name of each picture. Circle its name.

1. map nut nap mop	2. wax box boss tax
3. bill dull doll pill	4. sick sock sack suck
5. lot cab cot cat	6. pit pat pot got
7. lick lock luck lack	8. rid pod nod rod
9. top tap tip lip	10. fly box fox fog

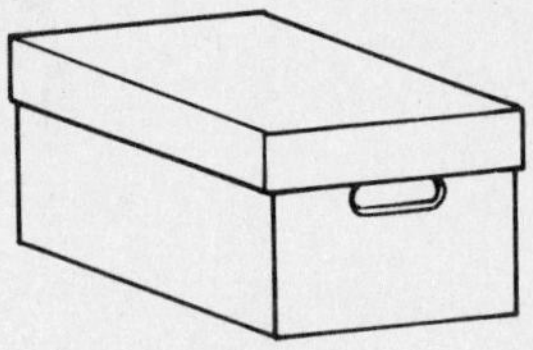

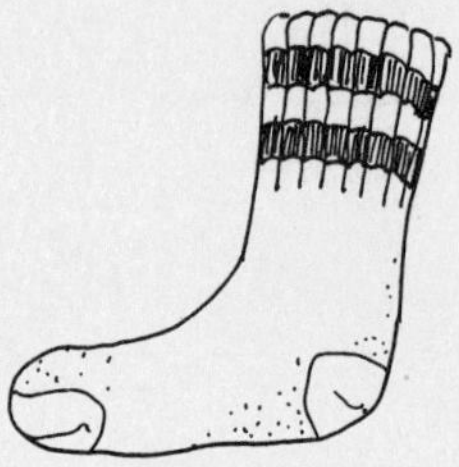

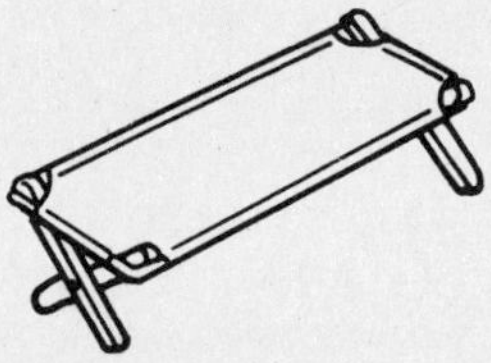

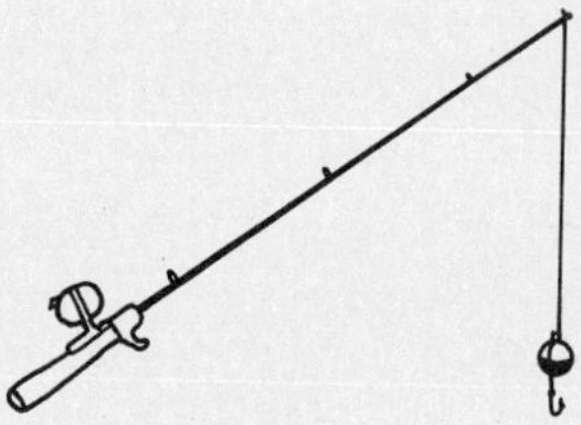

Short Vowel Sound: O

Say the name of each picture. Print the ending consonant of its name in the box.

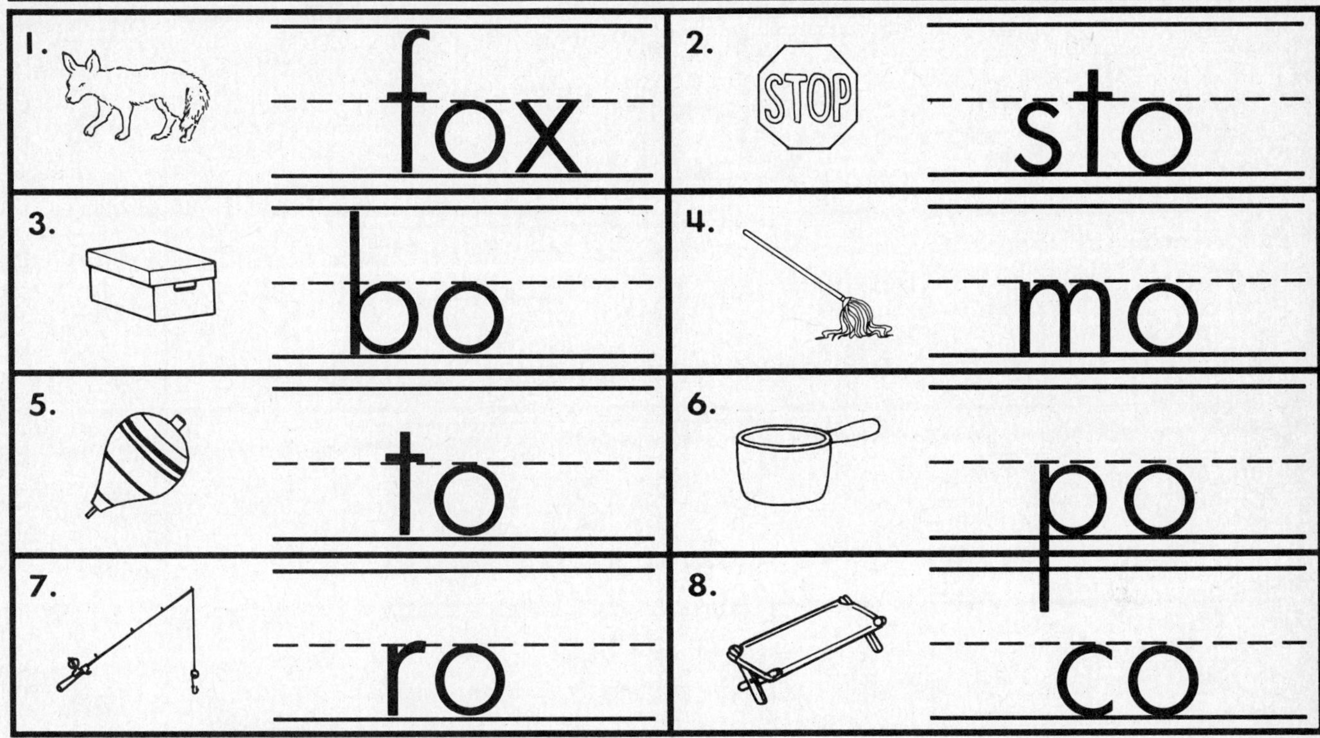

Say the name of each picture. Print the beginning and ending consonants of its name in the box.

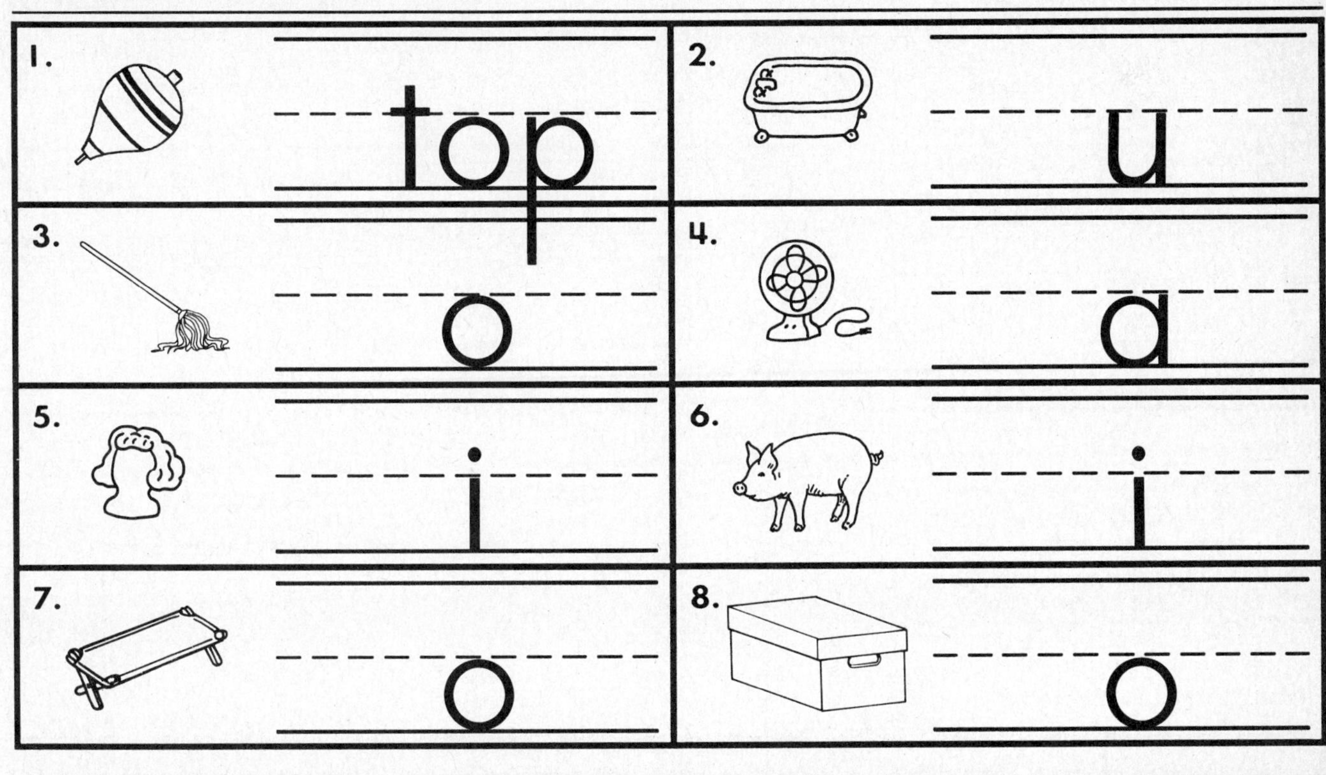

Short Vowel Sound: O

Look at the picture. Circle the word that will finish the sentence. The word you pick will be the name of the picture. Print the word in the box.

1.	Jill has a doll.	doll pal dill
2.	The man has a ________.	rid did rod
3.	You can fill the ________.	pan pin gun
4.	Dot will spin the ________.	lip top tap
5.	Tom hid the ________.	map mug mop
6.	The ham is in the ________.	pat pot pit
7.	Don will fill his ________.	cub nap cup
8.	Mom slept on a ________.	cat cot dot

Short Vowel Sound: O

Say the name of each picture. Print its name in the box.

1. fox	2.
3.	4.
5.	6.
7.	8.
9.	10.
11.	12.
13.	14.
15.	16.
17.	18.

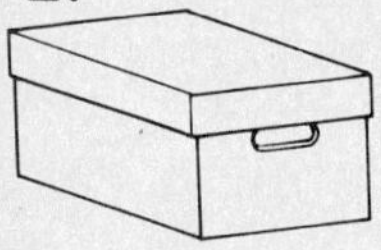

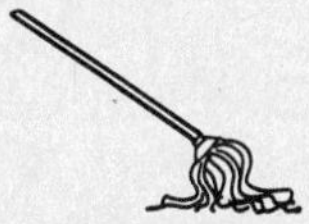

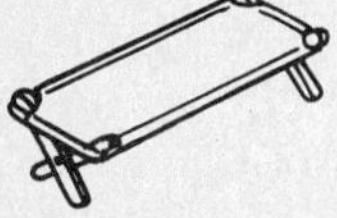

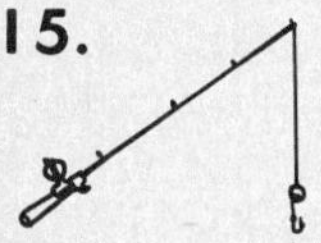

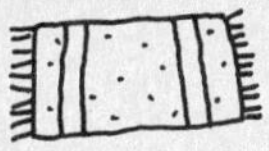

Short Vowel Sound: O

Read the words that are part of a sentence. Finish the sentence by writing the words from the box in the correct order.

1. You can lock the box.	lock box the
2. The cat can jump ______.	on the rocks
3. The tag is ______.	box the on
4. Dot can ______.	the lock fix
5. Jan will jump ______.	rock off the
6. The man ______.	the hid box
7. Don ______.	top the hid
8. Wags is ______.	pup a not

Short Vowel Sound: E

Say the name of each picture. If the name has the short sound of e, print e in the box.

1.  e	2. 	3. 
4. 	5. 	6. 
7. 	8. 	9. 
10. 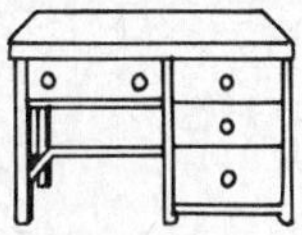	11. 	12. 

The word net has the short sound of e. Say the name of each picture. If the name has the short sound of e, circle the picture.

1. 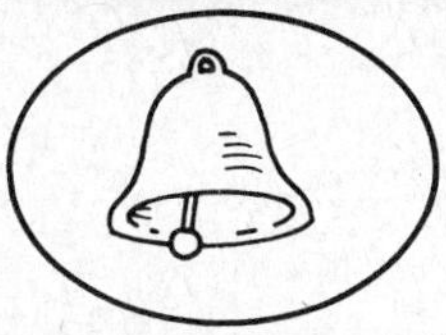	2. 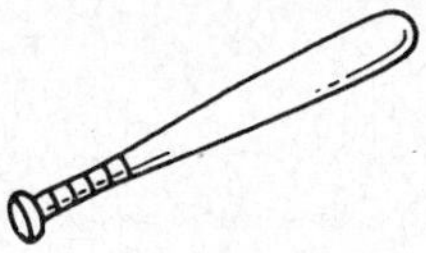	3. 	4. 
5. 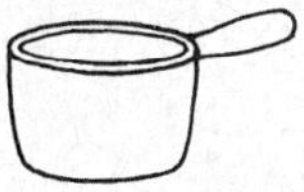	6. 	7. 	8. 
9. 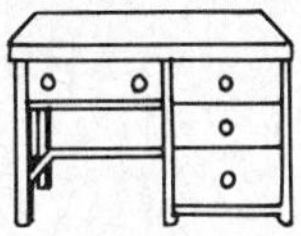	10. 	11. 	12. 
13. 	14. 	15. 	16. 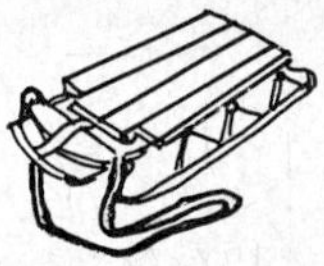

Short Vowel Sound: E

Say the name of each picture. If the name has the short sound of e, circle the picture.

1. 	2. 	3. 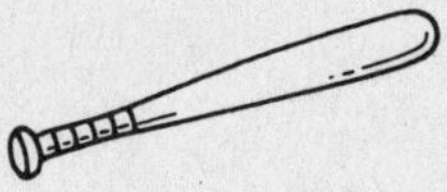	4. 
5. 	6. 	7. 	8. 
9. 	10. 	11. 	12. 
13. 	14. 	15. 	16. 

Say the name of each picture. Circle its name.

1.  pin pen pan	2. 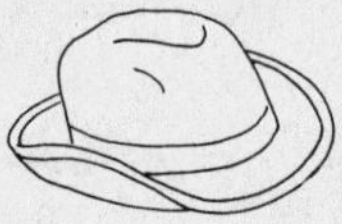 hit hot hat	3.  jet jam Jim
4.  pet pot pit	5. 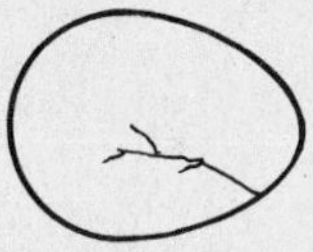 big beg egg	6.  bill bud bell
7.  desk disk dad	8.  not nut net	9.  man men met
10.  mat met mitt	11.  went web well	12.  bell well will

Short Vowel Sound: E

Say the name of each picture. Circle its name.

1. net nut not ten	2. wed win web rub
3. met mat mitt mad	4. ten tent tint sent
5. tell bell well bill	6. pin peg pen pan
7. beg big bag bug	8. hen hat hit ham
9. pit pot pet pat	10. bed bid bad bud

Short Vowel Sound: E

Say the name of each picture. Print the ending consonants of its name in the box.

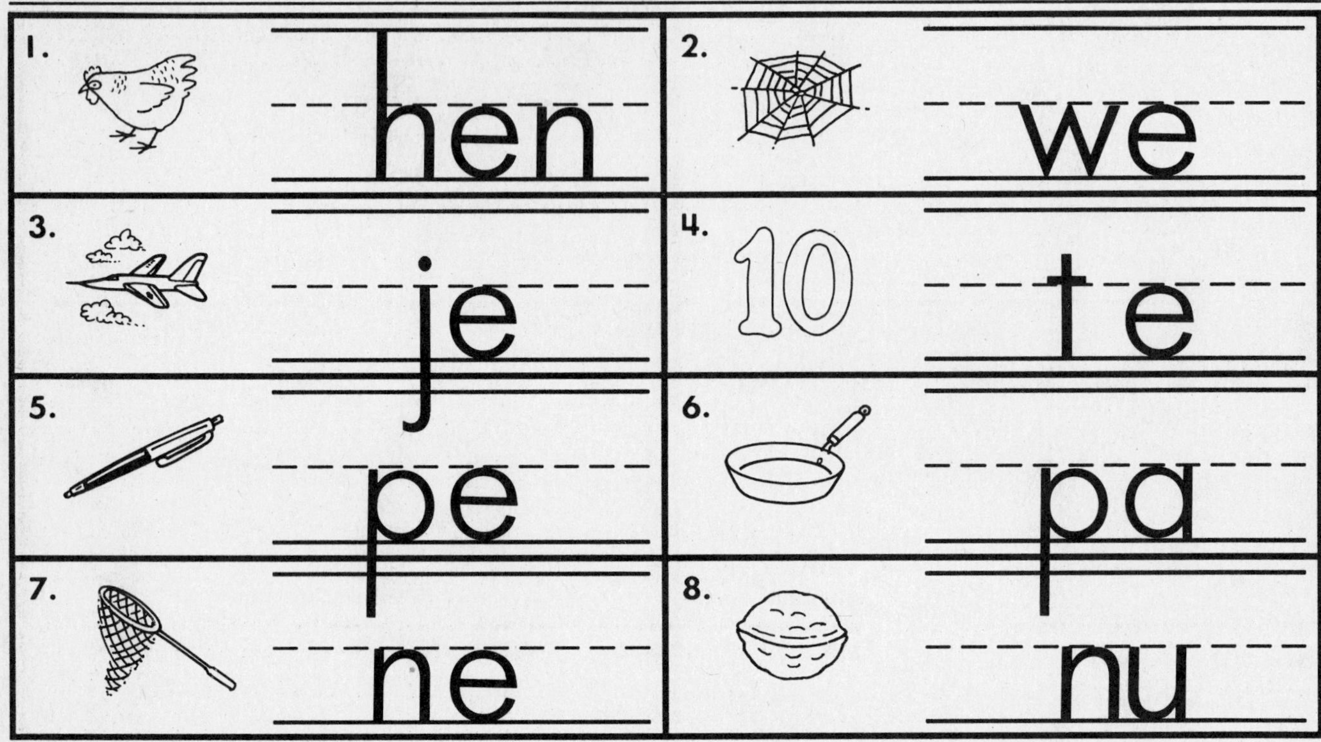

Say the name of each picture. Print the beginning and ending consonants of its name in the box.

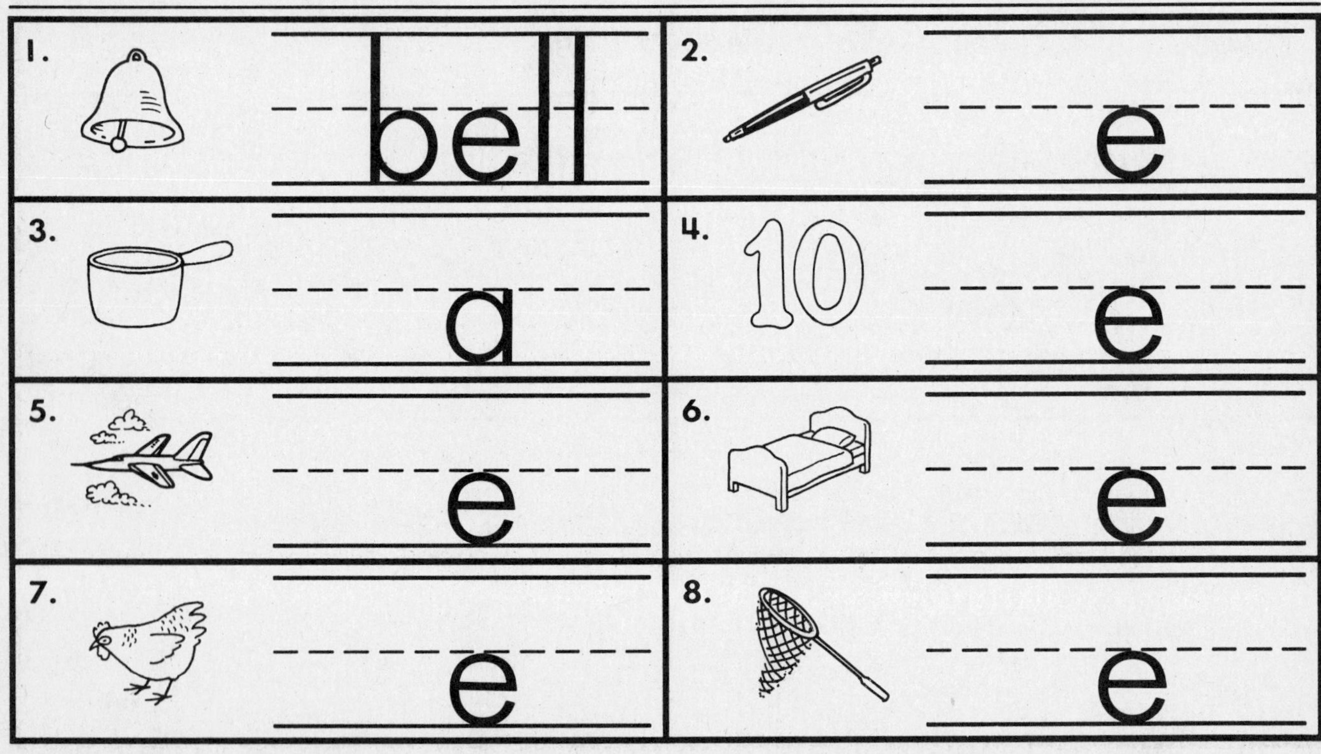

Short Vowel Sound: E

Look at the picture. Circle the word that will finish the sentence. The word you pick will be the name of the picture. Print the word in the box.

1.	Ted lent Ben his pen.	pan (pen) peg
2.	The red hen sat on the ______.	nest wet not
3.	Ben is sick in ______.	bad bed mat
4.	You can let Ted get the ______.	net bet met
5.	Bess fed the big fat ______.	hand hen hem
6.	Jen rang the ______.	bell belt bent
7.	Ten men got in the ______.	jet get got
8.	The bell fell in the ______.	web well will

Short Vowel Sound: E

Say the name of each picture. Print its name in the box.

1. jet	2.
3.	4.
5.	6.
7.	8.
9.	10.
11.	12.
13.	14.
15.	16.
17.	18.

Short Vowel Sound: E

Read the words that are part of a sentence. Finish the sentence by writing the words from the box in the correct order.

1. Pam has a big fat hen.	fat big hen
2. The hen sat ______.	nest the on
3. The men met ______.	on jet the
4. He did ______.	well his job
5. Ben ______.	bed to went
6. The hen sat ______.	tent the on
7. You can ______.	pet get a
8. Ten men ______.	got tent the

Review of Short Vowels

Play Tic-Tac-Toe. Draw a line through the three pictures in a row that have the same short vowel sound. You may find more than one row alike in a game.

1.

2.

3.

4.

Long Vowel Sound: A

Say the name of each picture. If the name has the long sound of a, print a in the box.

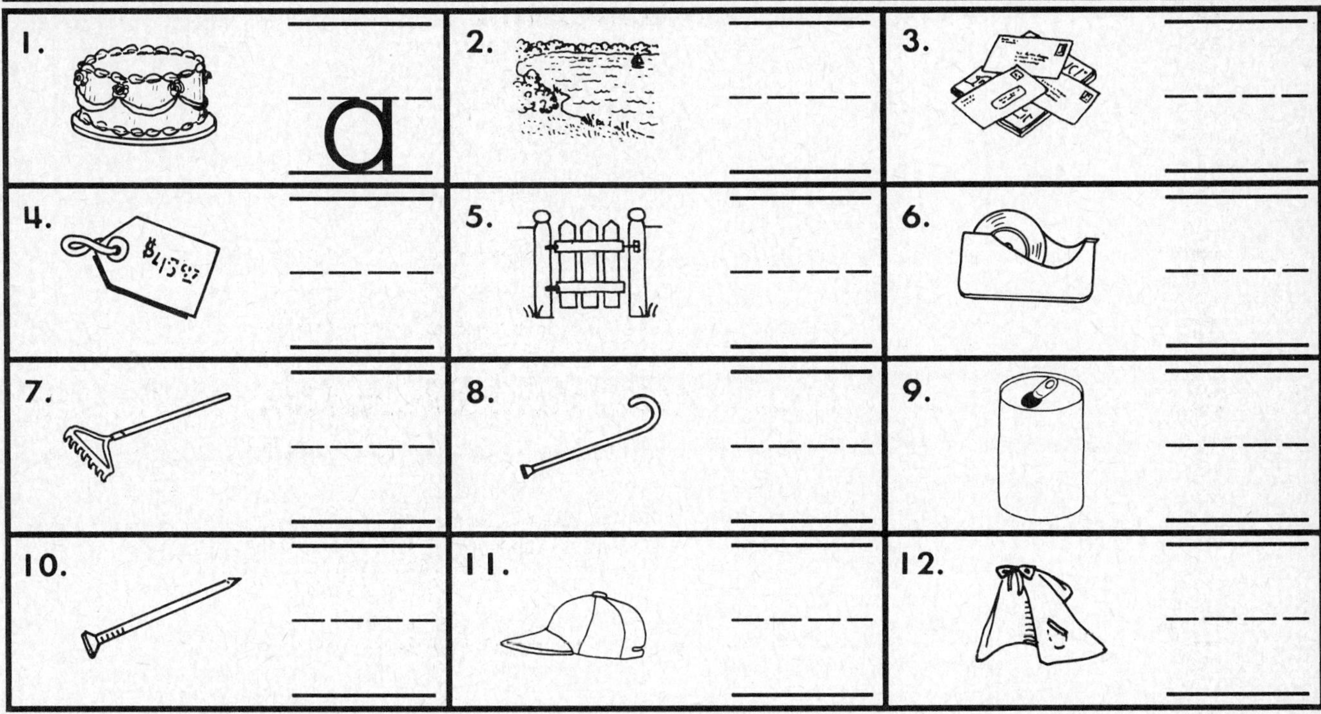

The word sail has the long sound of a. Say the name of each picture. If the name has the long sound of a, circle the picture.

1.	2.	3.	4.
5.	6.	7.	8.
9.	10.	11.	12.
13.	14.	15.	16.

Long Vowel Sound: A

Say the name of each picture. If the name has the long sound of a, circle the picture.

1. 	2. 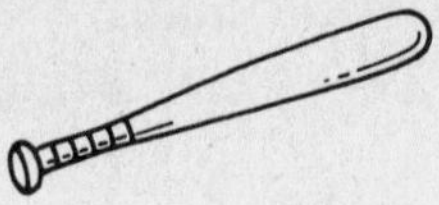	3. 	4. 
5. 	6. 	7. 	8. 
9. 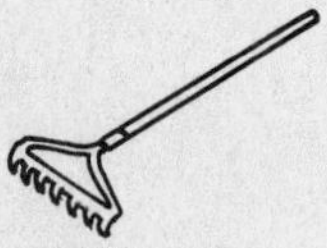	10. 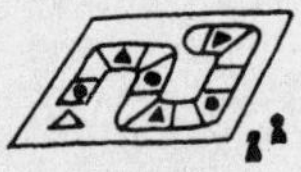	11. 	12. 
13. 	14. 	15. 	16. 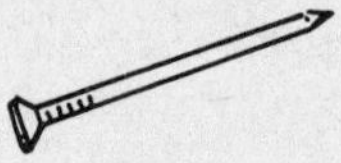

Say the name of each picture. Circle its name.

1. 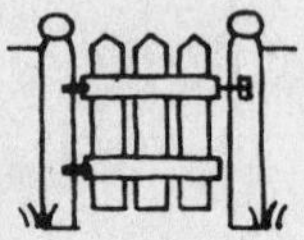 gate game gas	2.  cane cake cat	3.  tap tape tame
4.  nail maid mail	5. 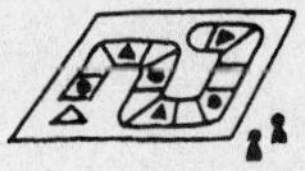 gas gate game	6. 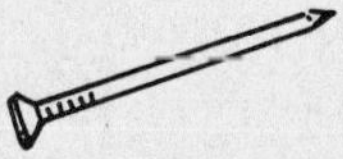 nail mane name
7. 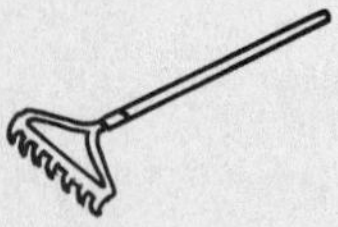 rate rake rack	8.  can cane came	9.  late lack lake
10.  sail sack sick	11.  rail rain ran	12.  vane van vase

Long Vowel Sound: A

Say the name of each picture. Circle its name.

1. rain ran rake run	2. late lame lack lake
3. tap tape pat tame	4. cat ate cape cap
5. gap gate pat cake	6. mail mat maid mad
7. vase save van vane	8. gas game gate gave
9. can cup cane cave	10. can cane cat cake

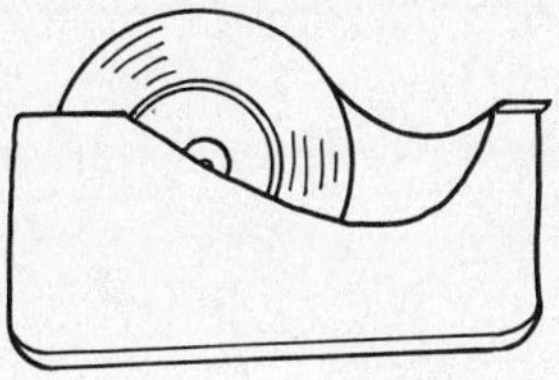

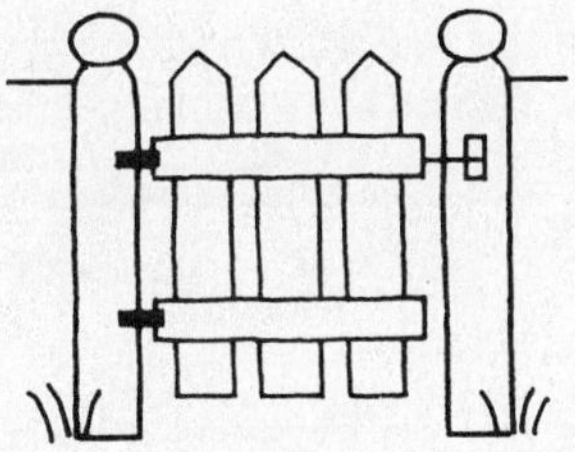

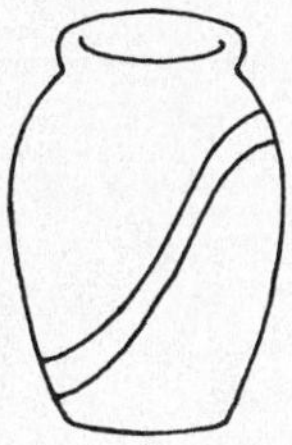

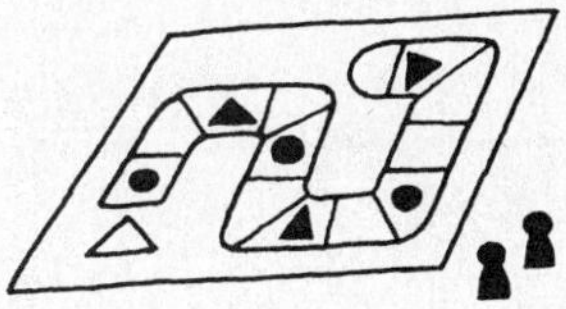

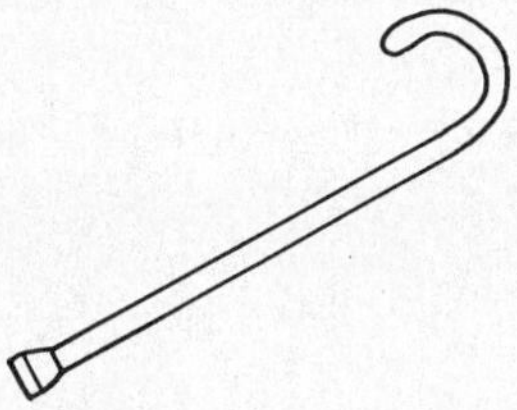

Long Vowel Sound: A

Say the name of each picture. Look at the word with the missing vowel. Print the missing vowel in the box.

1. cane	2. c n	3. j t
4. g te	5. c p	6. c pe
7. r ke	8. b t	9. m il
10. t b	11. r in	12. v se

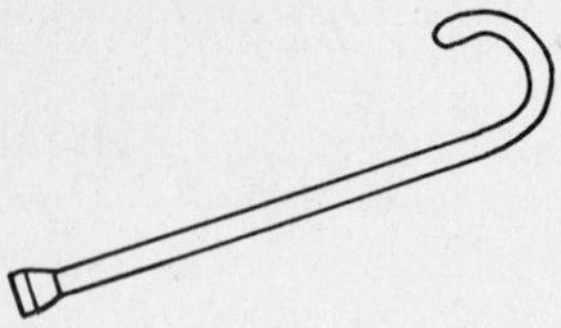

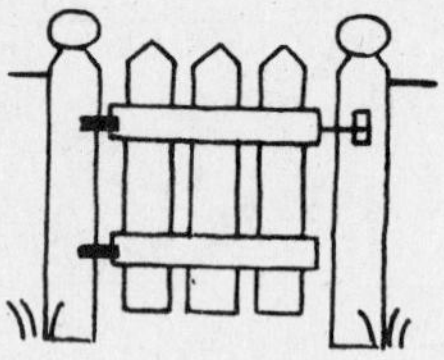

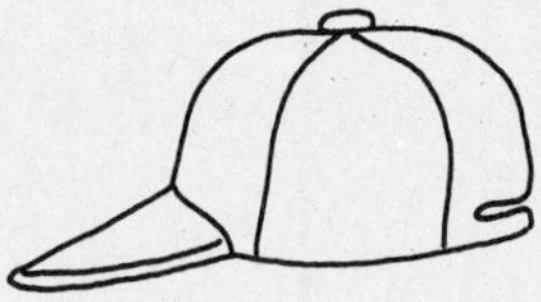

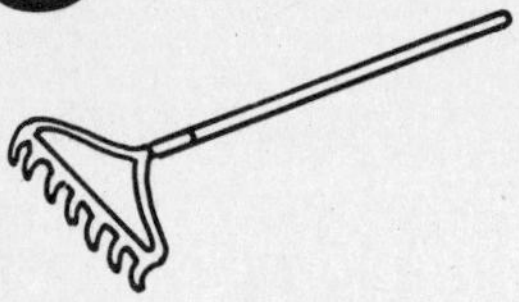

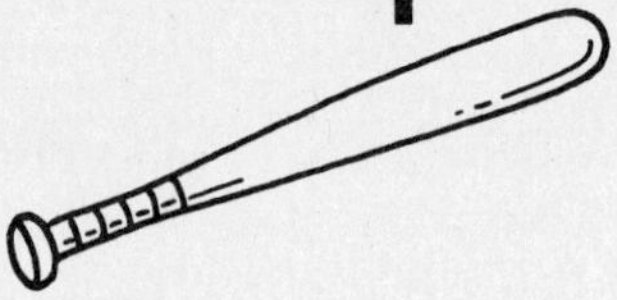

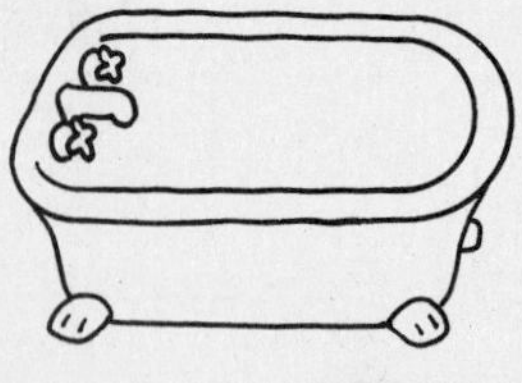

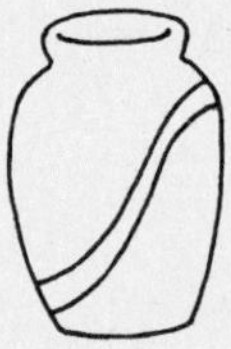

Long Vowel Sound: A

Look at the picture. Circle the word that will finish the sentence. The word you pick will be the name of the picture. Print the word in the box.

1. Dad gave Abe a game.	game (circled) gave gas
2. You can bake a ______.	cat cake cane
3. The box came in the ______.	maid mail nail
4. The dog will wag its ______.	tail take tag
5. Jill got wet in the ______.	ran rain rake
6. Sam hid in the ______.	came cake cave
7. Kate has a red ______.	cape cake can
8. Dad paid the man to ______.	rack rake rain

Long Vowel Sound: A

Say the name of each picture. Print its name in the box.

1. cape	2.
3.	4.
5.	6.
7.	8.
9.	10.
11.	12.
13.	14.
15.	16.
17.	18.

Long Vowel Sound: A

Read the words that are part of a sentence. Finish the sentence by writing the words from the box in the correct order.

1. Kate will not wait.	wait will not
2. Dave ran ______.	to lake the
3. Jake ______.	the ate cake
4. Can you ______?	fix the gate
5. Did the dog ______?	tail wag its
6. Sam hates to ______.	bed the make
7. The big dam will ______.	a make lake
8. Jane came and ______.	ham the ate

Long Vowel Sound: I

Say the name of each picture. If the name has the long sound of i, print i in the box.

1. i	2.	3.
4.	5.	6.
7.	8.	9.
10.	11.	12.

The word bike has the long sound of i. Say the name of each picture. If the name has the long sound of i, circle the picture.

1.	2.	3.	4.
5.	6.	7.	8.
9.	10.	11.	12.
13.	14.	15.	16.

Long vowel Sound: I

Say the name of each picture. If the name has the long sound of i, circle the picture.

1. 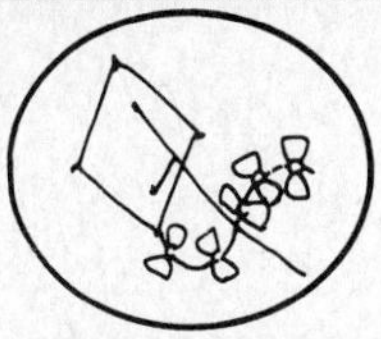	2. 	3. 	4. 
5. 	6. 	7. 	8. 
9. 	10. 	11. 	12. 
13. 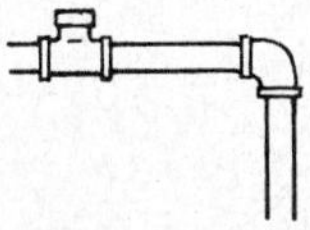	14. 	15. 	16. 

Say the name of each picture. Circle its name.

1. 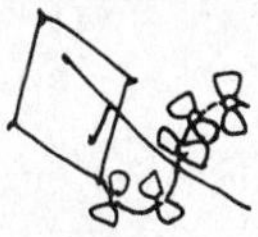 Kate kite kit	2.  pit pig pie	3.  rid ride ripe
4.  fire tire time	5. 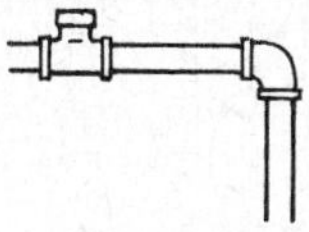 pine pie pipe	6.  hive have him
7.  tie tin tip	8.  bite bike kite	9.  nine mine vine
10.  dine dive dime	11. 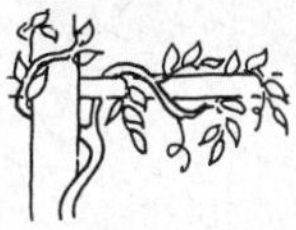 vine vane van	12.  fine five fire

Long Vowel Sound: I

Say the name of each picture. Circle its name.

1. hive hide hid hire	2. fire five wife fine
3. pie pipe pile pig	4. pin pie pine pipe
5. bite bike bit kite	6. ride rise ripe rip
7. vase van vine vane	8. dime dive dine dig
9. kit bite bit kite	10. fire fin five fine

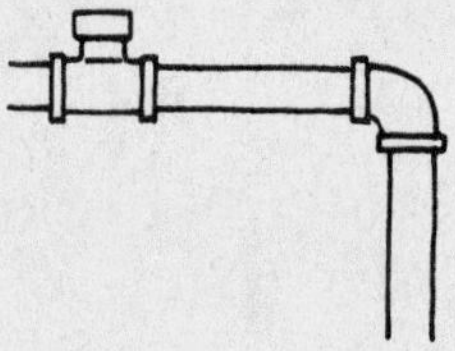

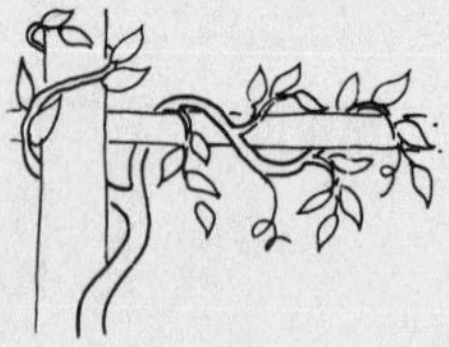

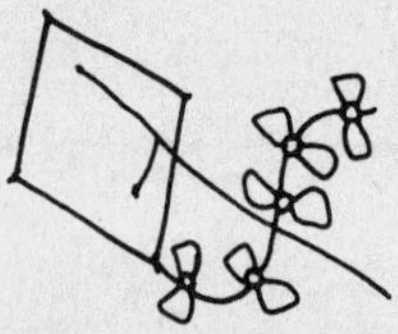

Long Vowel Sound: I

Say the name of each picture. Look at the word with the missing vowel. Print the missing vowel in the box.

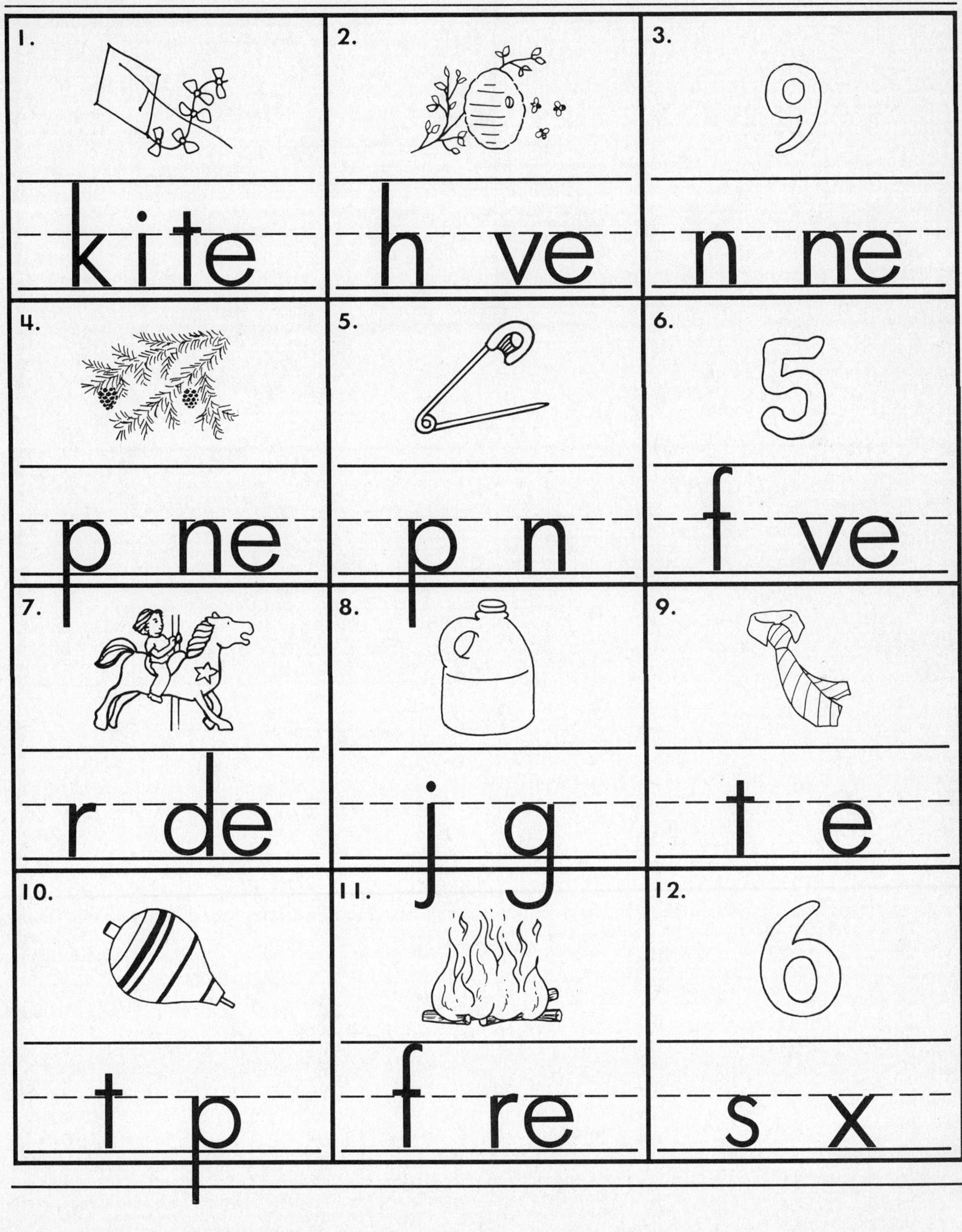

Long Vowel Sound: I

Look at the picture. Circle the word that will finish the sentence. The word you pick will be the name of the picture. Print the word in the box.

1. Bill hid the kite.	kit (kite) bite
2. Can you fix the ______?	time tin tire
3. Kate gave Dad a ______.	tie tip tin
4. Nate can ______.	dime dive dim
5. I like to ride a ______.	bike bit bite
6. Take time to make a ______.	fine fire five
7. Pat made a lime ______.	pie pig pit
8. It is fun to ______.	ride rid ripe

Long Vowel Sound: I

Say the name of each picture. Print its name in the box.

1. bike	2.
3.	4.
5.	6.
7.	8.
9.	10.
11.	12.
13.	14.
15.	16.
17.	18.

Long Vowel Sound: I

Read the words that are part of a sentence. Finish the sentence by writing the words from the box in the correct order.

1. Take time to bake a pie.	a pie bake
2. Did the rat ______________?	man the bite
3. Wipe the mud ______________.	bike off the
4. It is time to ______________.	pick limes the
5. Kim can ______________.	a mile hike
6. Nan will ______________.	hide dime the
7. Pam will ______________.	bake five pies
8. Mike can ______________.	bike his ride

Long Vowel Sound: U

Say the name of each picture. If the name has the long sound of u, print u in the box.

1.  u	2. 	3. 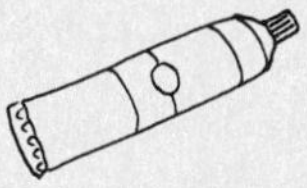
4. 	5. 	6. 
7. 	8. 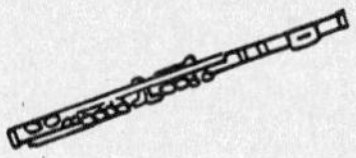	9. 
10. 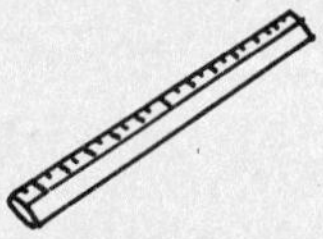	11. 	12. 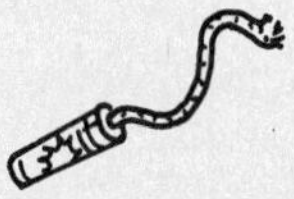

The word cube has the long sound of u. Say the name of each picture. If the name has the long sound of u, circle the picture.

1. 	2. 	3. 	4. 
5. 	6. 	7. 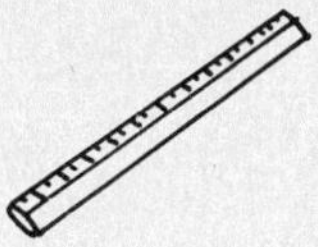	8. 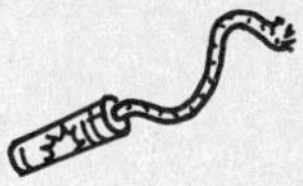
9. 	10. 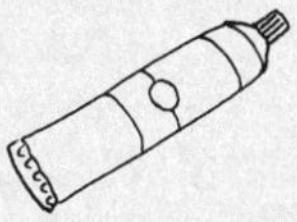	11. 	12. 
13. 	14. 	15. 	16. 

Long Vowel Sound: U

Say the name of each picture. If the name has the long sound of u, circle the picture.

1. 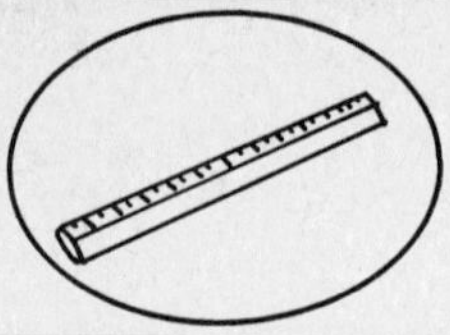	2. 	3. 	4. 
5. 	6. 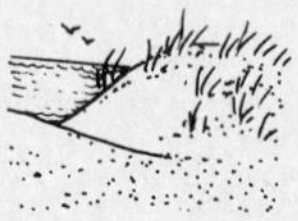	7. 	8. 
9. 	10. 	11. 	12. 
13. 	14. 	15. 	16. 

Say the name of each picture. Circle its name.

1. 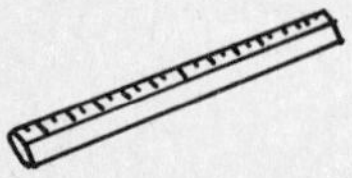 rule rude rug	2.  sun Sue suit	3. 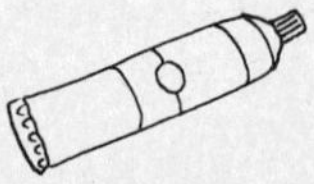 tub tube but
4.  mile male mule	5.  tub tube but	6.  luck bus fuss
7.  but bug big	8.  cut cub cube	9.  but bud bat
10.  tune jute June	11.  cub cut tub	12. 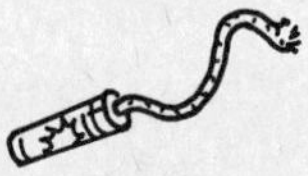 fuss fuse fan

Long Vowel Sound: U

Say the name of each picture. Circle its name.

1. mule, tune, male, mile	2. cub, cube, cup, cut
3. jump, jute, June, tune	4. flute, lure, rude, rug
5. tube, tub, tab, but	6. but, tab, tub, tube
7. Sue, suit, sit, sun	8. cube, cab, lure, cub
9. fuss, fuse, fun, fin	10. tube, tune, tin, tub

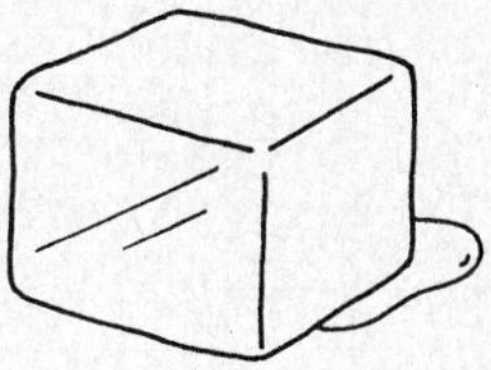

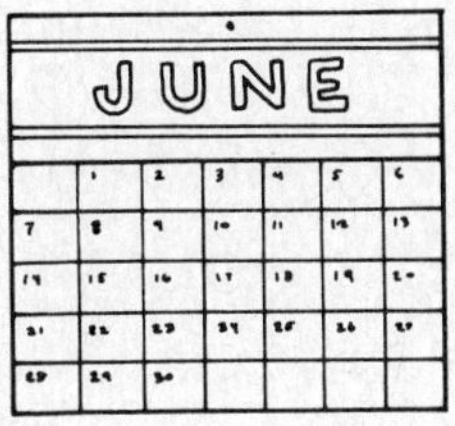

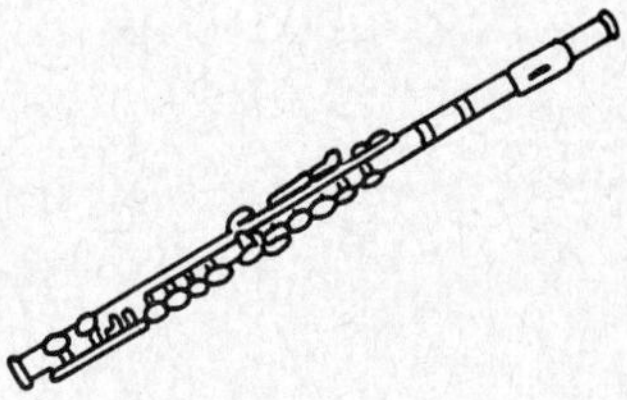

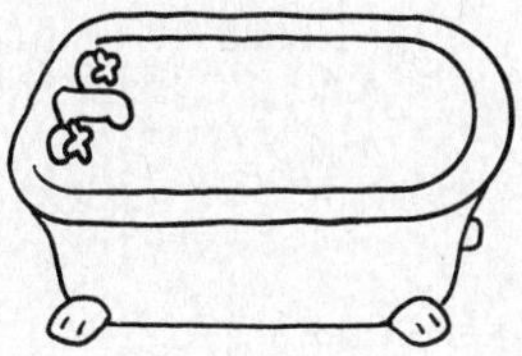

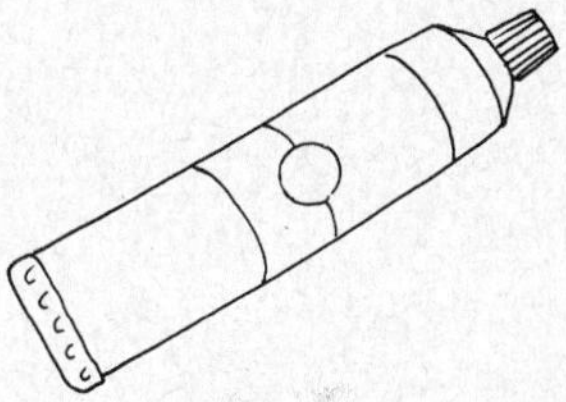

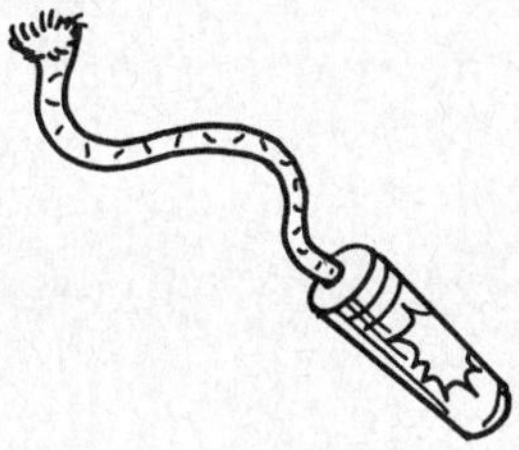

Long Vowel Sound: U

Say the name of each picture. Look at the word with the missing vowel. Print the missing vowel in the box.

1. mule	2. b x	3. fl te
4. c be	5. c p	6. h n
7. t b	8. t be	9. f se
10. w g	11. s n	12. b s

Long Vowel Sound: U

Look at the picture. Circle the word that will finish the sentence. The word you pick will be the name of the picture. Print the word in the box.

1.	Luke will play the flute.	(flute) sit stone
2.	Did Sue ride the ________?	rule mule mile
3.	Mike went on a trip to the ________.	tunes dimes dunes
4.	Sue got the cape last ________.	June jute tune
5.	Jack has a new ________.	suit sit sun
6.	He has a ________ in his cup.	cute cub cube
7.	Can you pass me the ________?	tube tub but
8.	Will you hum a ________?	tame tube tune

Long Vowel Sound: U

Look at the word in each box. If you hear a short vowel sound, circle s. If you hear a long vowel sound, circle l.

1. cube s (l)	2. lake s l	3. dim s l
4. cub s l	5. dime s l	6. fuse s l
7. tune s l	8. fuss s l	9. tube s l
10. paid s l	11. mule s l	12. bag s l

Say the name of each picture. Print its name in the box.

1. fuse	2.
3.	4.
5.	6.
7.	8.

Long Vowel Sound: U

Read the words that are part of a sentence. Finish the sentence by writing the words from the box in the correct order.

1. Dad gave a mule to June.	to mule June
2. Jane ______.	fuse the lit
3. Did Jack ______?	use bat the
4. Luke will ______.	tune a hum
5. Duke will ______.	mule the ride
6. Make a line ______.	with ruler the
7. The fat ______.	pup cute is
8. The dog has fun ______.	with the mule

Long Vowel Sound: O

Say the name of each picture. If the name has the long sound of o, print o in the box.

1.  O	2. 	3. 
4. 	5. 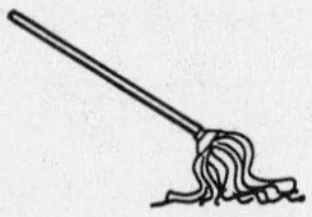	6. 
7. 	8. 	9. 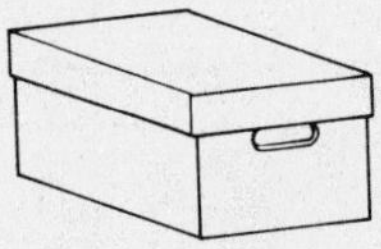
10. 	11. 	12. 

The word hose has the long sound of o. Say the name of each picture. If the name has the long sound of o, circle the picture.

1. 	2. 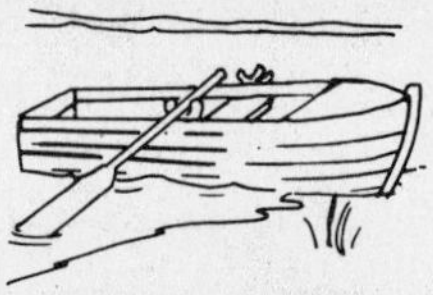	3. 	4. 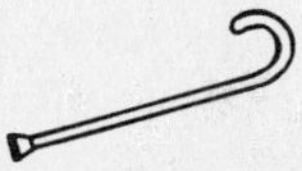
5. 	6. 	7. 	8. 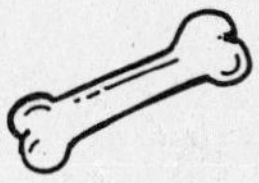
9. 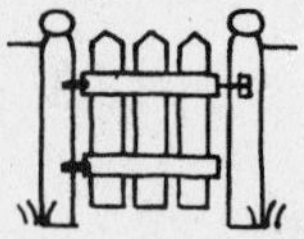	10. 	11. 	12. 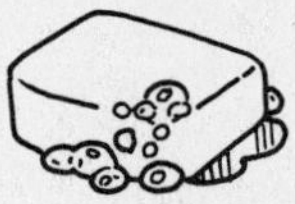
13. 	14. 	15. 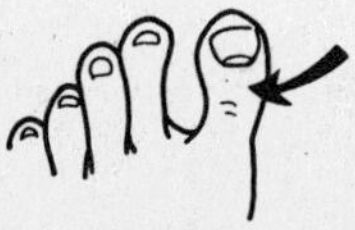	16. 

Long Vowel Sound: O

Say the name of each picture. If the name has the long sound of o, circle the picture.

1. 	2. 	3. 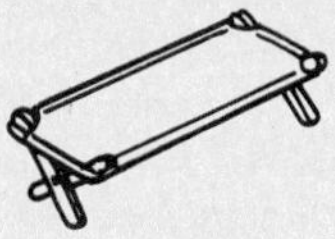	4. 
5. 	6. 	7. 	8. 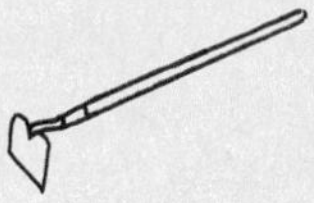
9. 	10. 	11. 	12. 
13. 	14. 	15. 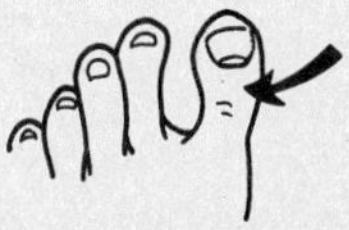	16. 

Say the name of each picture. Circle its name.

1.  dose dome Dom	2.  cone cane can	3. 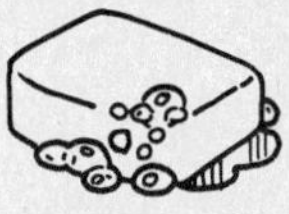 soak soap pose
4.  tone note nose	5.  road rod robe	6. 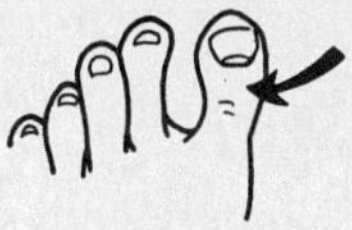 tie top toe
7.  robe rob road	8.  got goat goal	9.  Tod toad tone
10.  boat bun bone	11.  hop hoe hug	12.  coat cot cute

Long Vowel Sound: O

Say the name of each picture. Circle its name.

1. rose (circled) rise road rod	2. bat boat bone but
3. rose ripe rap rope	4. rod robe road rob
5. top tap toe tie	6. load toad tune tone
7. pose soak sun soap	8. bun bone bin boat
9. nose note not sand	10. home hop hole hoe

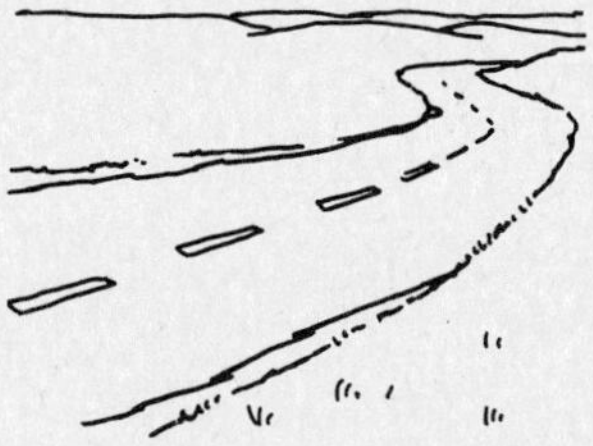

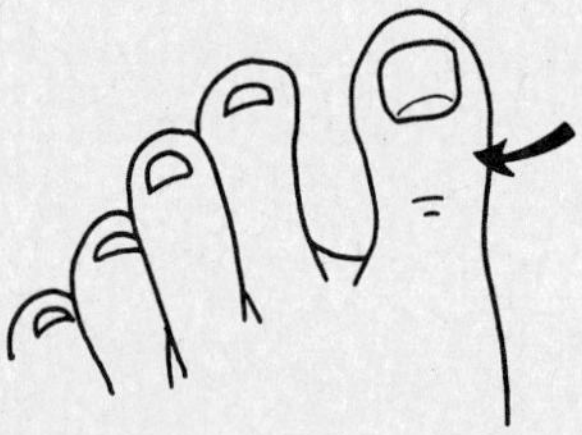

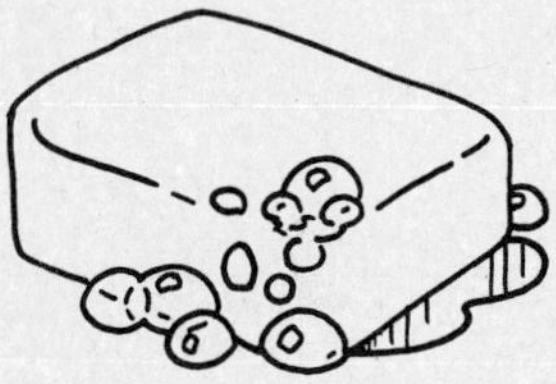

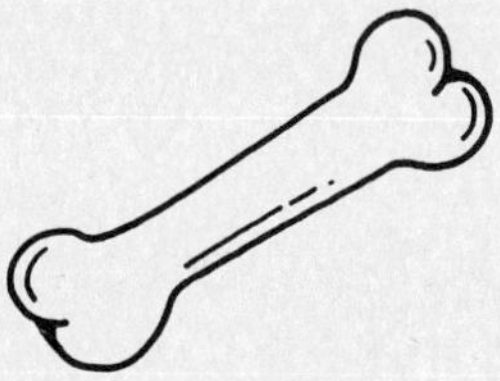

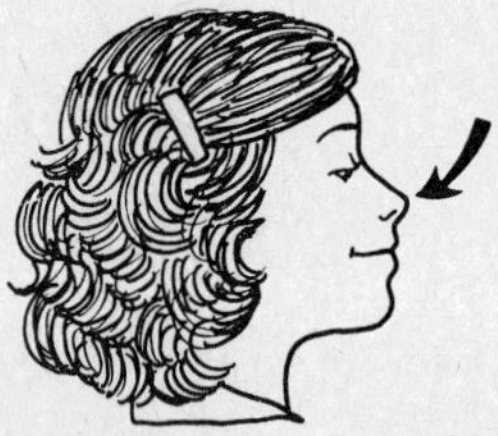

Long Vowel Sound: O

Say the name of each picture. Look at the word with the missing vowel. Print the missing vowel in the box.

1. rope	2. h e	3. c t
4. b ne	5. b d	6. n se
7. r be	8. d me	9. m p
10. r ad	11. r in	12. g at

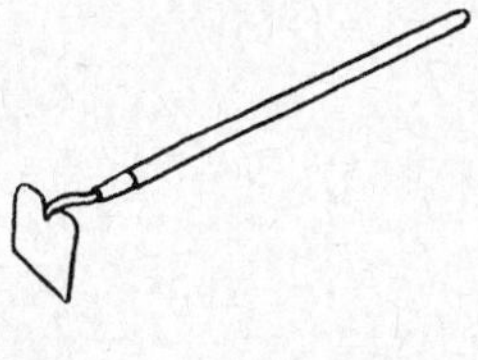

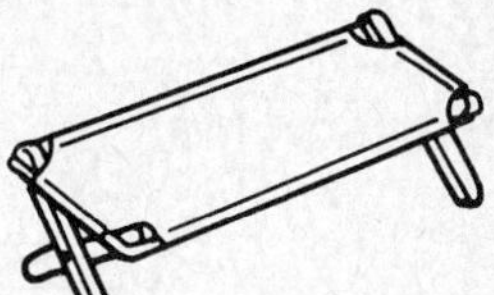

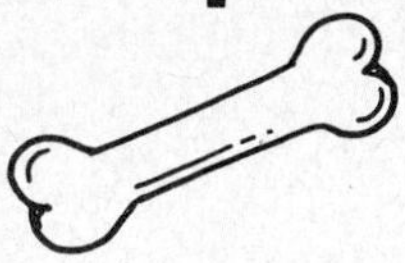

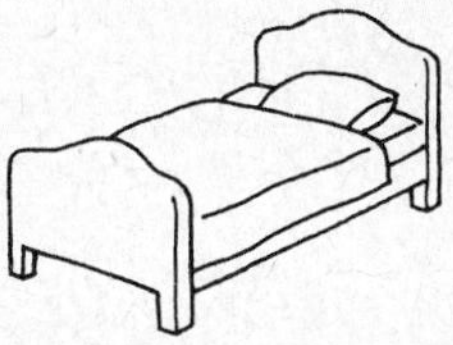

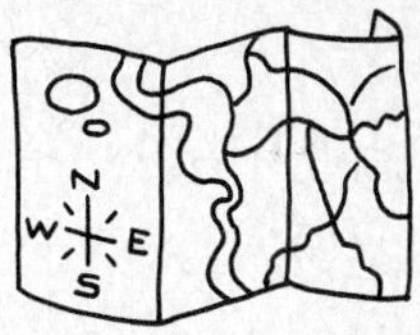

Long Vowel Sound: O

Look at the picture. Circle the word that will finish the sentence. The word you pick will be the name of the picture. Print the word in the box.

1.	Bob cut his big toe.	top (toe) ten
2.	Give Joan the big red ____.	rose rug road
3.	The ____ is near the pond.	Tod toad tone
4.	The bug bit Duke on the ____	nose note net
5.	Use the ____ to fill the pail.	hose hoe home
6.	The ____ ate the cone.	got goat goal
7.	Toss the dog a ____.	bone bin boat
8.	Use a rope to tie up the ____.	bone bat boat

Long Vowel Sound: O

Say the name of each picture. Print its name in the box.

1. boat	2.
3.	4.
5.	6.
7.	8.
9.	10.
11.	12.
13.	14.
15.	16.
17.	18.

Long Vowel Sound: E

Read the words that are part of a sentence. Finish the sentence by writing the words from the box in the correct order.

1. Joe can make a goal.	make goal a
2. I can get ________.	at home six
3. Ann has ________.	coat cute a
4. Tim will tell ________.	Ann a joke
5. Joan rode ________.	a in boat
6. Did you ________?	the hoe use
7. The dog ________.	hid bone its
8. Tie the bell ________.	on goat the

Long Vowel Sound: E

Say the name of each picture. If the name has the long sound of e, print e in the box.

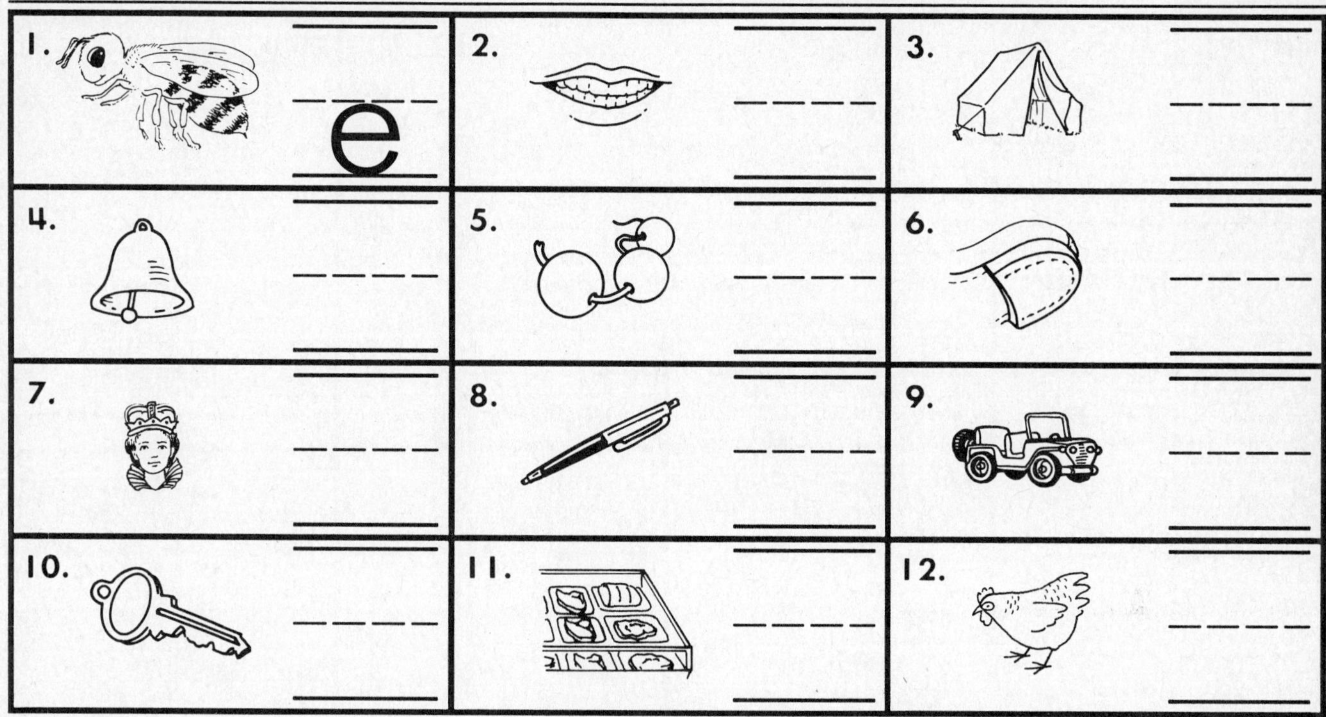

The word heel has the long sound of e. Say the name of each picture. If the name has the long sound of e, circle the picture.

1.	2.	3.	4.
5.	6.	7.	8.
9.	10.	11.	12.
13.	14.	15.	16.

Long Vowel Sound: E

Say the name of each picture. If the name has the long sound of e, circle the picture.

1. 	2. 	3. 	4. 
5. 	6. 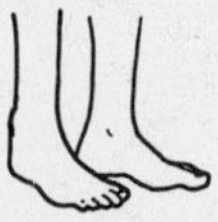	7. 	8. 
9. 	10. 	11. 	12. 
13. 	14. 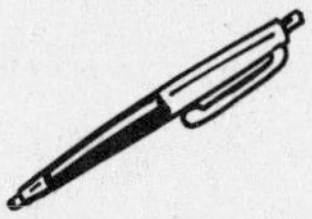	15. 	16. 

Say the name of each picture. Circle its name.

1.  beet bet beak	2.  set seed seat	3. 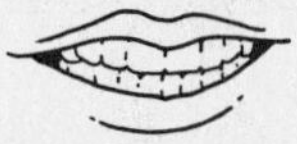 ten meet teeth
4.  peep jeep jet	5.  heel heat hen	6.  meat met team
7.  seal sell seat	8.  beans beads beds	9.  bean bee bead
10.  left leaf feel	11.  weep wed weed	12. 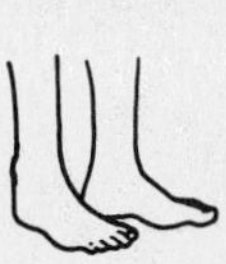 feet feel fed

Long Vowel Sound: E

Say the name of each picture. Circle its name.

1. heat hen hole heel	2. jeep peep Jean jet
3. sell seat seal seed	4. team met mean meat
5. bead beet bet beak	6. beans beads bites boats
7. feet feel leaf fed	8. beets beads beds beans
9. set seal sell seat	10. lead left leaf feel

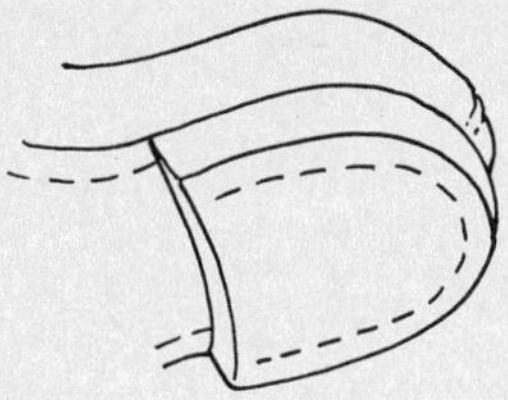

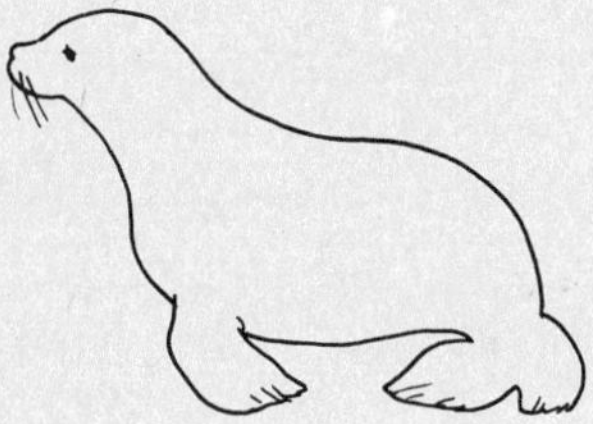

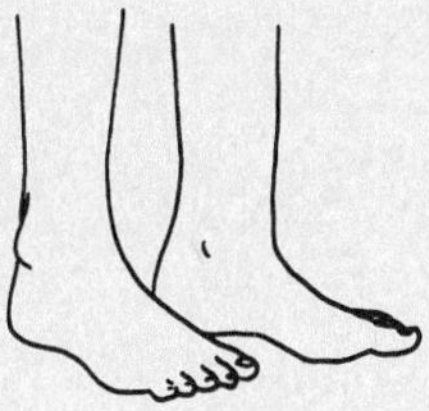

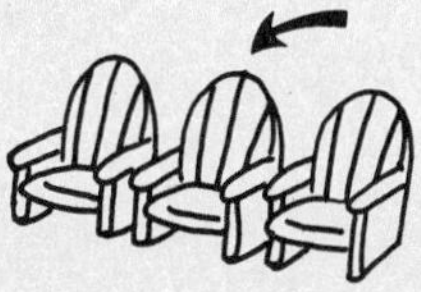

Long Vowel Sound: E

Say the name of each picture. Look at the word with the missing vowel. Print the missing vowel in the box.

1. h el	2. b g	3. f et
4. f x	5. j ep	6. s al
7. l af	8. s at	9. p g
10. b t	11. b d	12. b e

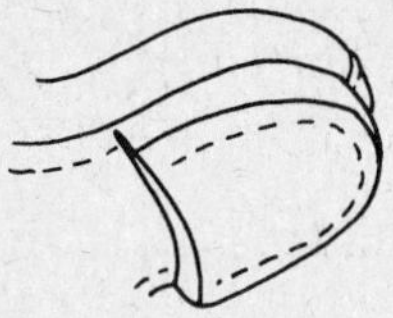

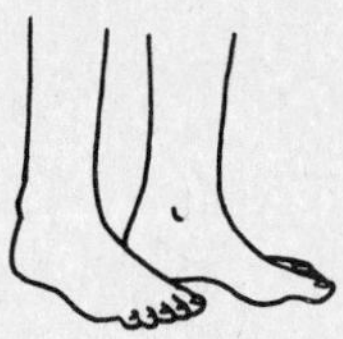

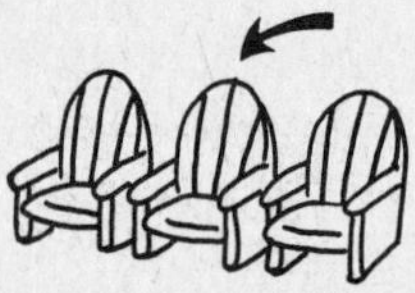

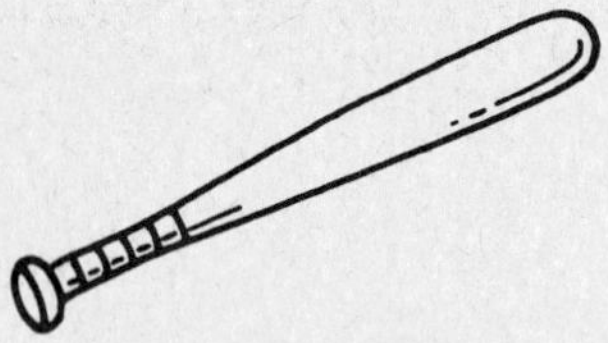

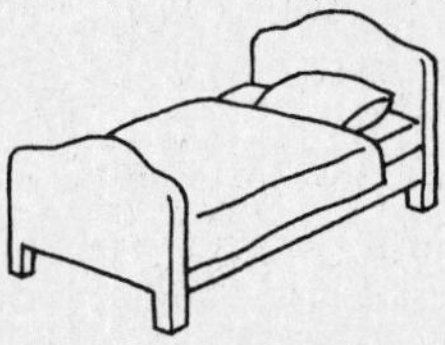

LONG VOWEL SOUND: E

Look at the picture. Circle the word that will finish the sentence. The word you pick will be the name of the picture. Print the word in the box.

1. Pete has gum on his heel.	hen, (heel), heat
2. The man will fix my ______.	teeth, pets, ten
3. We rode in the ______.	Jean, jet, jeep
4. A hive is the home of the ______.	bead, bean, bee
5. A ______ fell in the lake.	leak, leaf, let
6. The name of the ______ is Tess.	sell, seat, seal
7. The man has big hands and ______.	feet, fed, feel
8. Duke had ______ to eat.	met, meat, team

Long Vowel Sound: E

Say the name of each picture. Print its name in the box.

1. leaf	2.
3.	4.
5.	6.
7.	8.
9.	10.
11.	12.
13.	14.
15.	16.
17.	18.

Long Vowel Sound: E

Read the words that are part of a sentence. Finish the sentence by writing the words from the box in the correct order.

1. See the goat eat the hat.	hat eat the
2. The bee is ______.	the on leaf
3. See the hive ______.	of the bee
4. Jean rode ______.	jeep the in
5. Dean is ______.	seat his in
6. The cat is ______.	in tree the
7. Ted will wade ______.	the sea in
8. The hen pecks ______.	at seed the

Review of Vowels

Look at the picture. Circle the word that will finish the sentence. The word you pick will be the name of the picture. Print the word in the box.

1.	I will pin a note on your coat.	coat cot code
2.	A duck bit the tail of the ______.	ax box fox
3.	Jane can dive in the ______.	lack lake late
4.	Will Mike make his ______?	bed bad belt
5.	The gift will be on his ______.	set seat seal
6.	Jack and Jill went up the ______.	bill hill pill
7.	The red ______ will eat the seed.	his him hen
8.	Sue will ride the big ______.	bus bun bud

Review of Vowels

Say the name of each picture. Print its name in the box.

1. cot	2.
3.	4.
5.	6.
7.	8.
9.	10.
11.	12.
13.	14.
15.	16.
17.	18. 10

Review of Vowels

Read the words that are part of a sentence. Finish the sentence by writing the words from the box in the correct order.

1. Wipe your feet on the mat.	mat on the
2. The game is ______________.	in the box
3. The tame ______________.	mule fast ran
4. Take an ax to ______________.	tree cut the
5. Hide the map ______________.	den the in
6. Sue gave the ______________.	to key Ann
7. Mike has pie ______________.	bib his on
8. Use ropes to ______________.	load the tie

Word Ending: S

Say the name of each picture. Circle its name.

1. tack (tacks)	2. nail nails	3. nine nines
4. cone cones	5. goat goats	6. cat cats
7. rod rods	8. sock socks	9. rose roses
10. pig pigs	11. cake cakes	12. mule mules

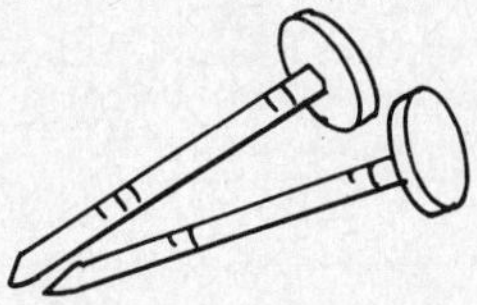

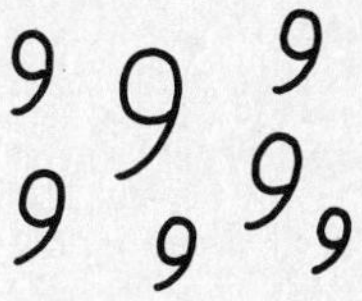

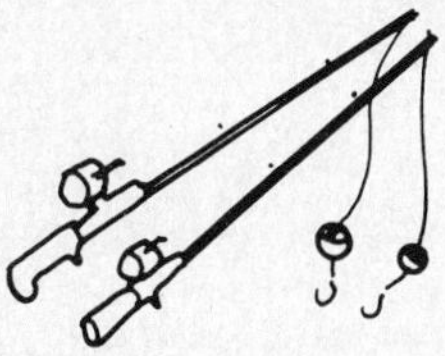

Word Ending: ED Sounded as ED

The word melted is melt + ed. Melt is the base word of melted and ed is the word ending. Circle each base word below. Print the base word in the box.

1. melted melt	2. seated
3. needed	4. loaded
5. heated	6. painted
7. weeded	8. baited

Read the words that are part of a sentence. Circle the word that will finish the sentence. Print the word in the box.

1. The bus is loaded .	load loaded
2. Jim is ________ in the rear.	seat seated
3. We like to ________ to see Jane.	waited wait
4. The boat ________ a sail.	needed need

Word Ending: ED Sounded as T

The word soaped is soap + ed. Soap is the base word and ed is the word ending. In soaped, ed has the sound of t. Circle each base word below. Print the base word in the box.

1. locked — lock	2. passed
3. picked	4. ticked
5. fixed	6. peeped
7. loafed	8. mixed

Read the words that are part of a sentence. Circle the word that will finish the sentence. Print the word in the box.

1. Jan locked the gate.	lock / locked
2. Tom ______ a rose to Nell.	toss / tossed
3. I will ______ the beans in a pan.	soak / soaked
4. Jeff ______ up his hat.	picked / pick

Word Ending: ED Sounded as D

The word mailed is mail + ed. Mail is the base word and ed is the word ending. In mailed, ed has the sound of d. Circle each base word below. Print the base word in the box.

1. filled	fill	2. foamed	
3. nailed		4. leaned	
5. peeled		6. feared	
7. rained		8. sailed	

Read the words that are part of a sentence. Circle the word that will finish the sentence. Print the word in the box.

1. We sailed on the lake.	sails sailed
2. The sick man ______.	moan moaned
3. June ______ her plate.	filled fill
4. Joe ______ his dog.	train trained

Word Ending: ING

The word nailing is nail + ing. Nail is the base word of nailing and ing is the word ending. Circle each base word below. Print the base word in the box.

1. waiting wait	2. seating
3. soaking	4. passing
5. boxing	6. winking
7. reading	8. ticking

Read the words that are part of a sentence. Circle the word that will finish the sentence. Print the word in the box.

1. I think reading is fun.	read reading
2. We will ______ a cake.	mix mixing
3. Mom is ______ the tent.	fix fixing
4. The big boat is ______.	sink sinking

R Blends

The word train begins with the sound of tr. Say the name of each picture. If the name begins with the sound of tr, print tr in the box.

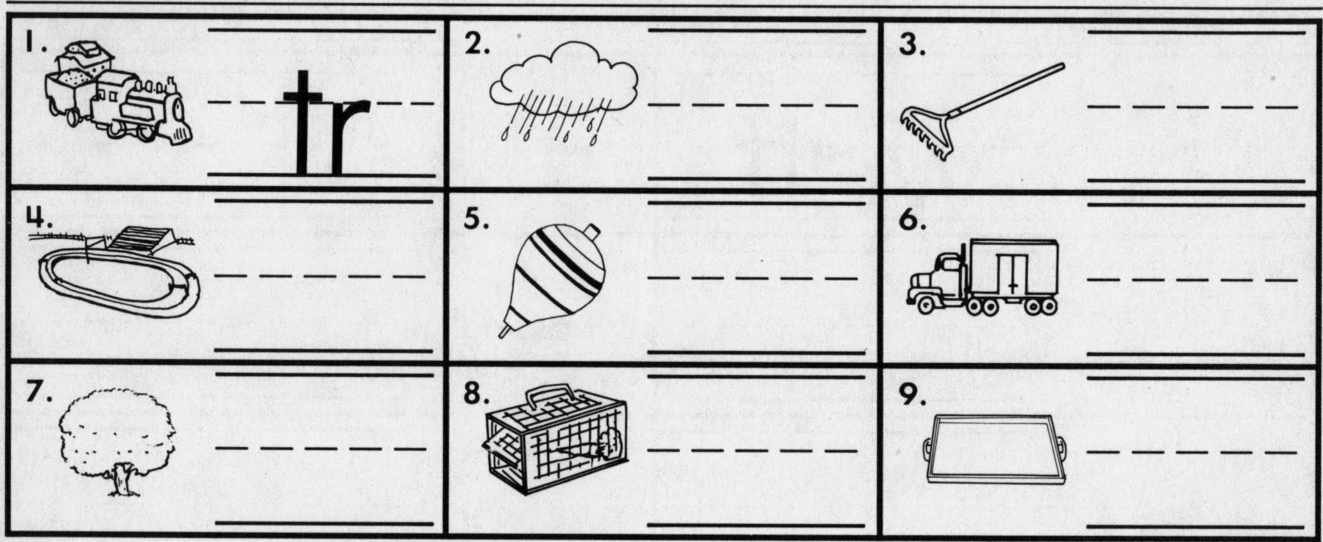

The word grass begins with the sound of gr. Say the name of each picture. If the name begins with the sound of gr, print gr in the box.

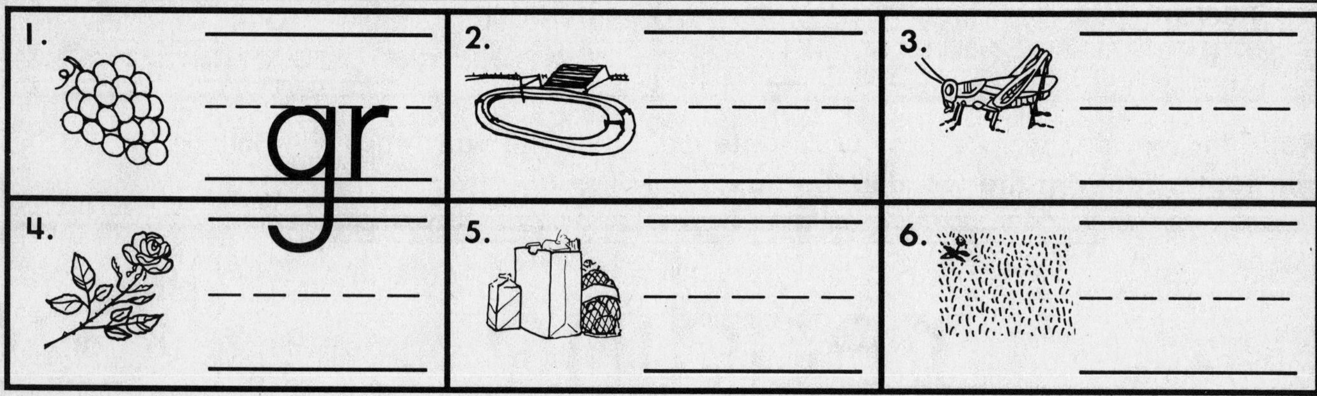

The word brick begins with the sound of br. Say the name of each picture. If the name begins with the sound of br, print br in the box.

1. br	2.	3.
4.	5.	6.

R Blends

The word prize begins with the sound of pr. Say the name of each picture. If the name begins with the sound of pr, print pr in the box.

The word cry begins with the sound of cr. Say the name of each picture. If the name begins with the sound of cr, print cr in the box.

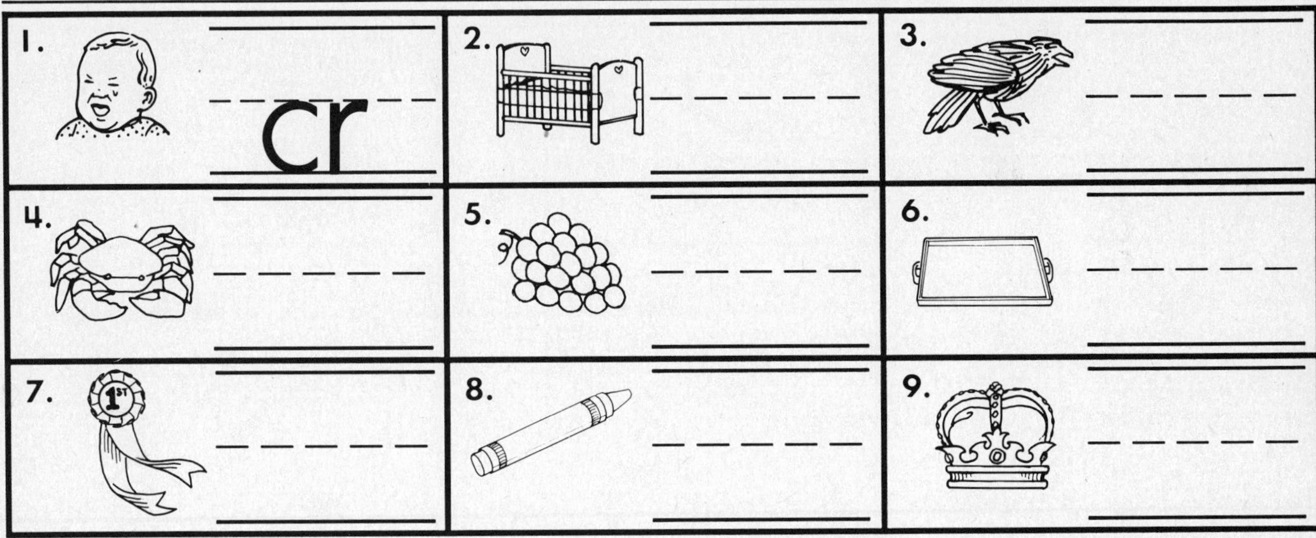

The word frog begins with the sound of fr. Say the name of each picture. If the name begins with the sound of fr, print fr in the box.

R Blends

The word dress begins with the sound of dr. Say the name of each picture. If the name begins with the sound of dr, print dr in the box.

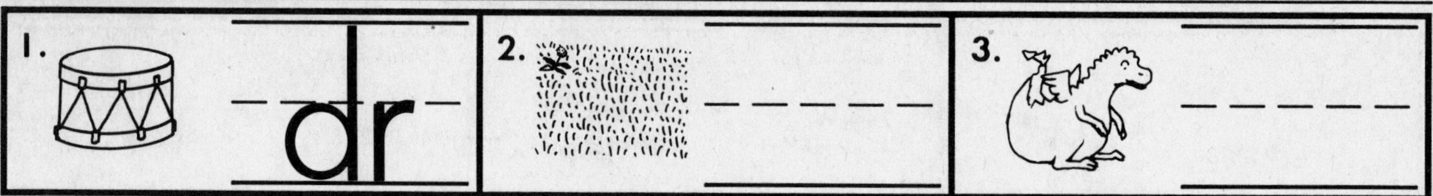

Say the name of each picture. Circle its name.

1. drum trump	2. trap grab	3. dries prize
4. drapes grapes	5. hog frog	6. brick trick
7. track crack	8. free tree	9. crown down
10. press dress	11. crib grab	12. train tray

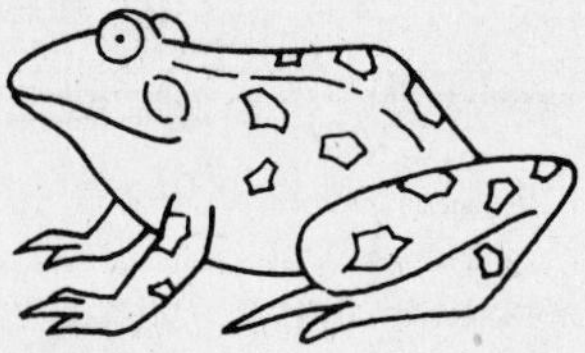

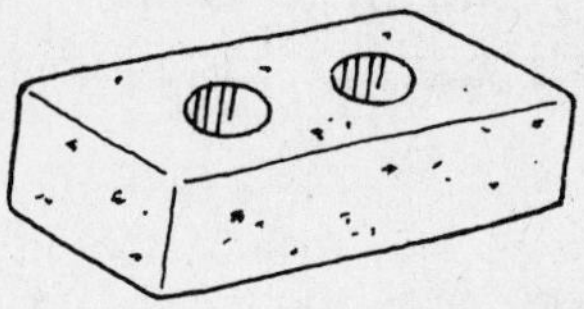

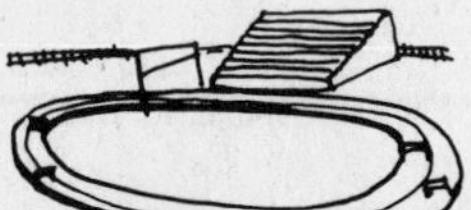

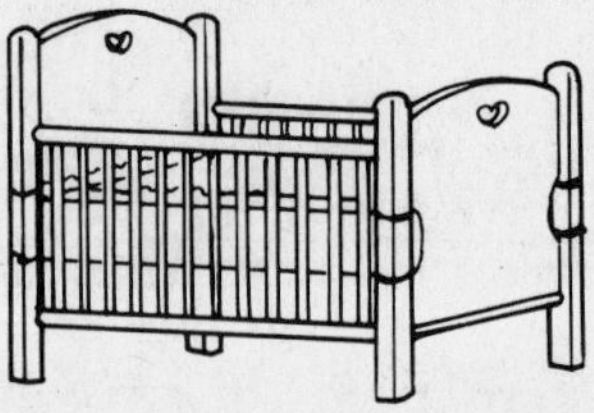

R Blends

Read the words that are part of a sentence. Circle the word that will finish the sentence. Print the word in the box.

1. Bob wins the prize .	cries prize dries
2. Fran had a pet ______ .	truck brick frog
3. A leaf fell off the ______ .	free tree trip
4. The ______ bit Sam on the toe.	crab drab grab
5. We will set the rat ______ .	trap trip drip
6. The ______ had a load of coal.	trick crack truck
7. Brad gave the ______ to Jane.	grapes grips cracks
8. The ______ has a pink dress.	prize bride braid

L Blends

The word clown begins with the sound of cl. Say the name of each picture. If the name begins with the sound of cl, print cl in the box .

The word blade begins with the sound of bl. Say the name of each picture. If the name begins with the sound of bl, print bl in the box.

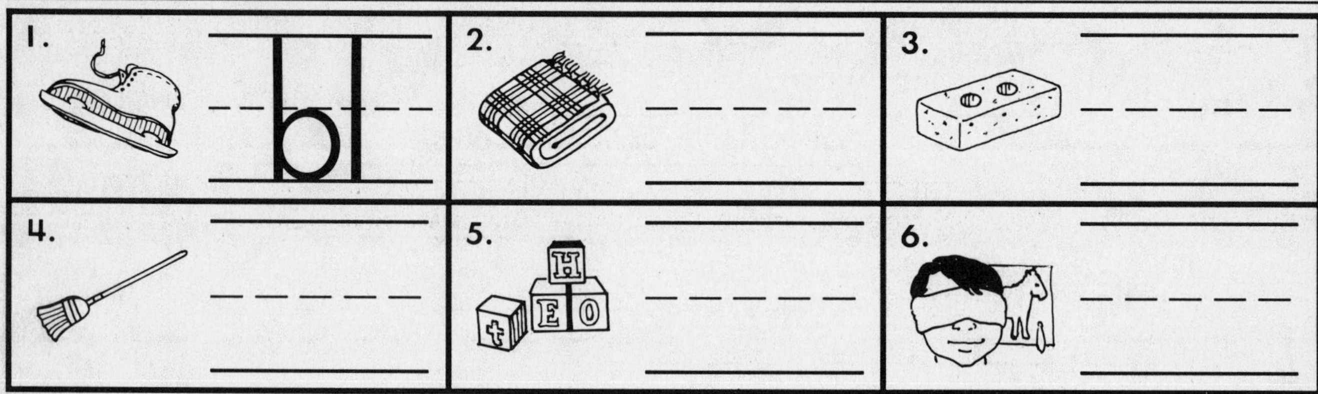

The word plate begins with the sound of pl. Say the name of each picture. If the name begins with the sound of pl, print pl in the box.

1. pl	2.	3.
4.	5.	6.

L Blends

The word flag begins with the sound of fl. Say the name of each picture. If the name begins with the sound of fl, print fl in the box.

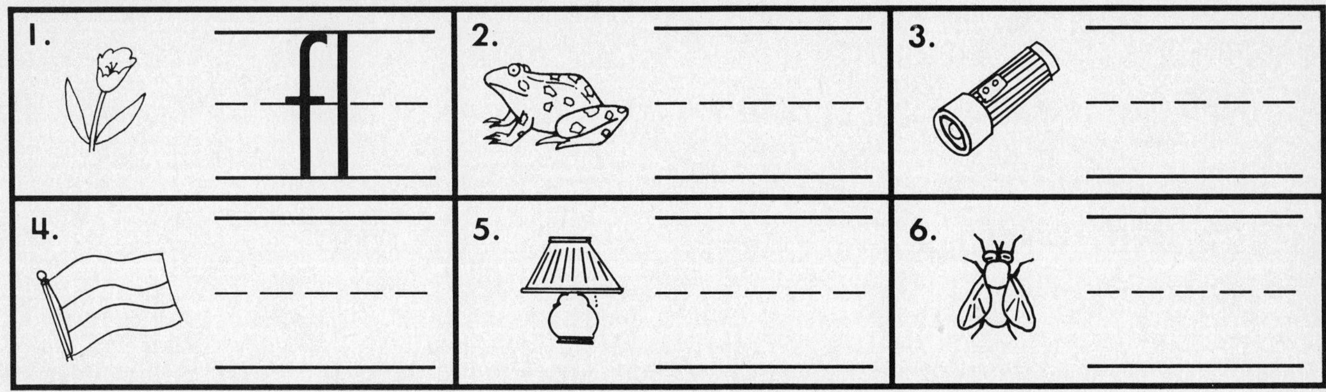

The word glue begins with the sound of gl. Say the name of each picture. If the name begins with the sound of gl, print gl in the box.

The name of each picture begins with the sound of bl, cl, fl, gl, or pl. Say the name of each picture. Print the letters of the beginning blend in the box.

L Blends

Say the name of each picture. Circle its name.

1. clap flap	2. plug bug	3. glue blue
4. glad flag	5. clock block	6. block clock
7. glow glove	8. plant blend	9. globe clove
10. glass class	11. plate late	12. ply fly

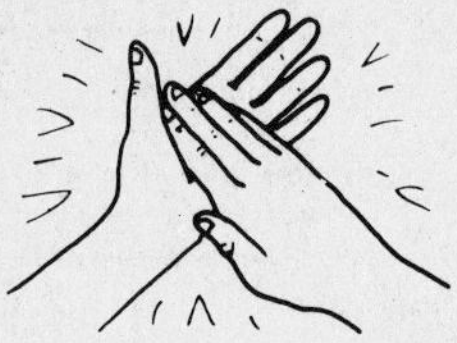

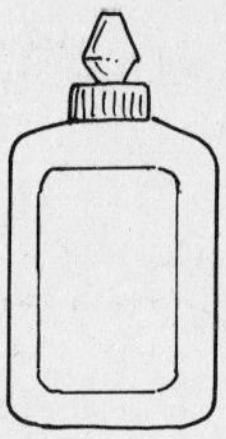

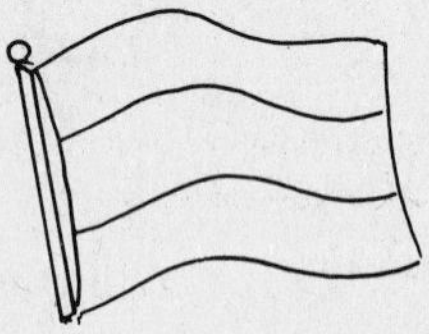

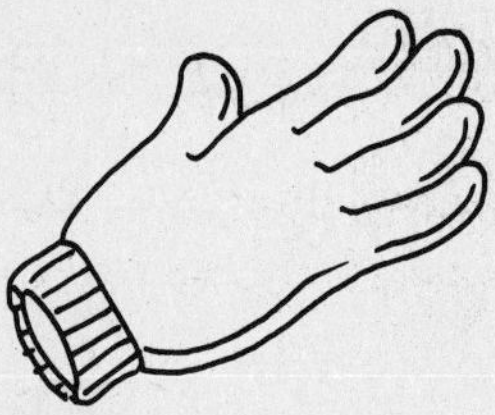

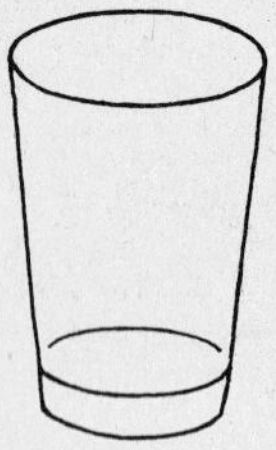

L Blends

Read the words that are part of a sentence. Circle the word that will finish the sentence. Print the word in the box.

1. Please clean the glass.	(clean) mean clap
2. The desk top is ________.	plant glad flat
3. Do not let the ________ drip.	plan glue glad
4. The whole ________ can print well.	clap class blast
5. We can ________ beans here.	clay plate plant
6. The ________ tells us the time.	block lock clock
7. The ________ flies on the top of the pole.	brag drag flag
8. The ________ dress fits Jane.	block blue blank

S Blends

The word sled begins with the sound of sl. Say the name of each picture. If the name begins with the sound of sl, print sl in the box.

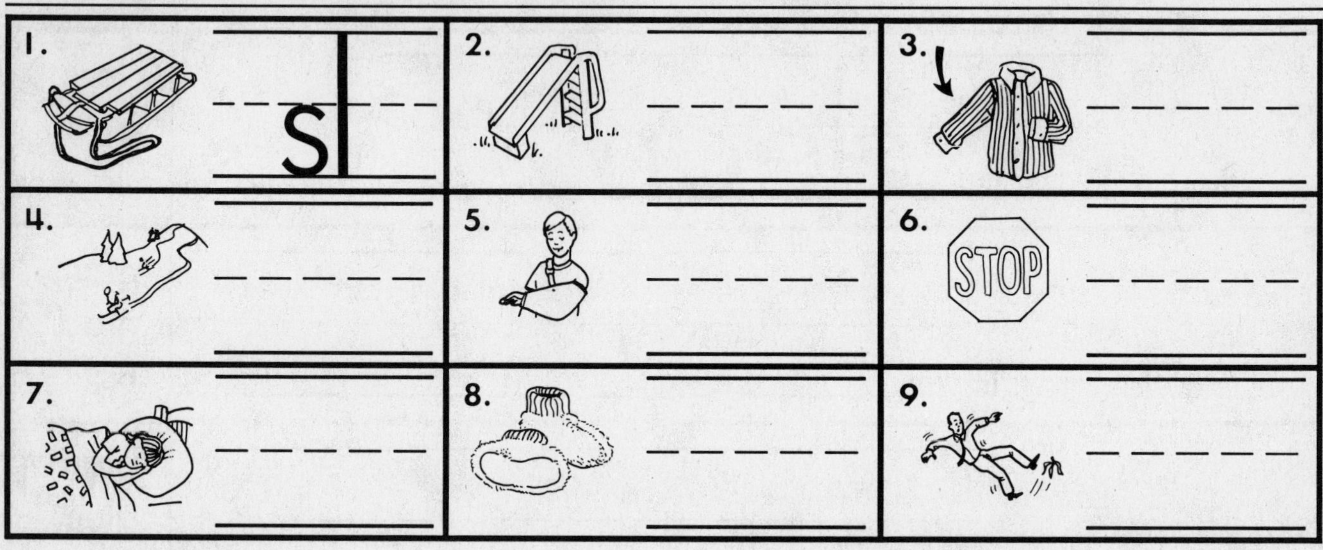

The word smoke begins with the sound of sm. Say the name of each picture. If the name begins with the sound of sm, print sm in the box.

The word steps begins with the sound of st. Say the name of each picture. If the name begins with the sound of st, print st in the box.

1. st	2.	3.
4.	5.	6.

S Blends

The word spider begins with the sound of sp. Say the name of each picture. If the name begins with the sound of sp, print sp in the box.

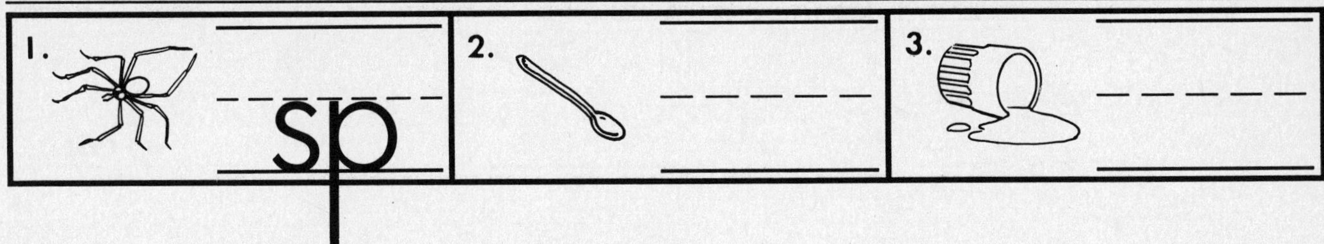

The word scold begins with the sound of sc. Say the name of each picture. If the name begins with the sound of sc, print sc in the box.

The word snail begins with the sound of sn. Say the name of each picture. If the name begins with the sound of sn, print sn in the box.

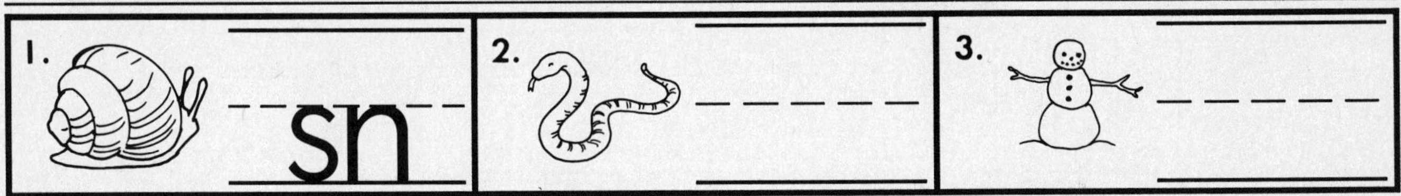

The word skate begins with the sound of sk. Say the name of each picture. If the name begins with the sound of sk, print sk in the box.

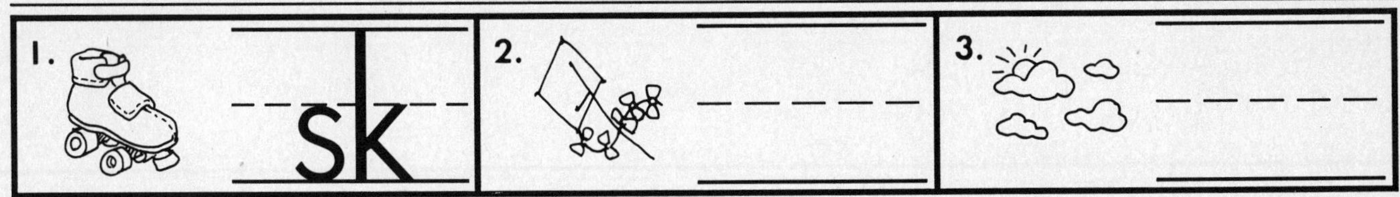

The word swim begins with the sound of sw. Say the name of each picture. If the name begins with the sound of sw, print sw in the box.

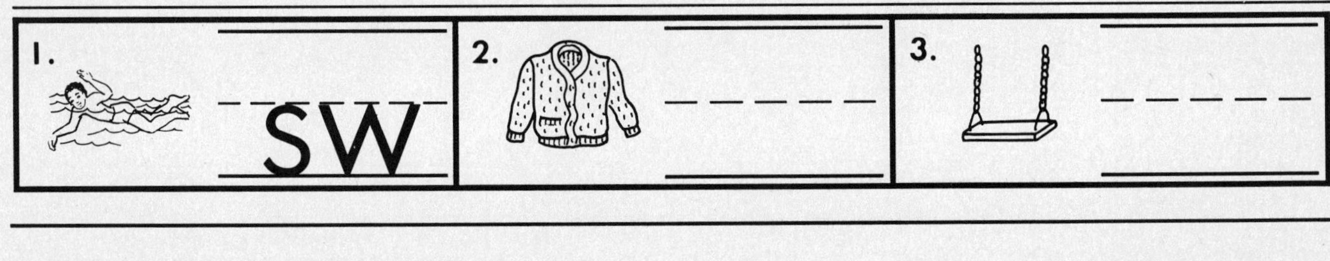

S Blends

The word scrub begins with the sound of scr. Say the name of each picture. If the name begins with the sound of scr, print scr in the box.

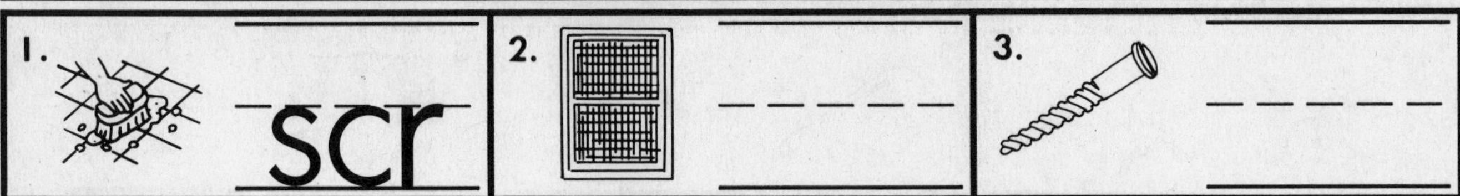

The word split begins with the sound of spl. Say the name of each picture. If the name begins with the sound of spl, print spl in the box.

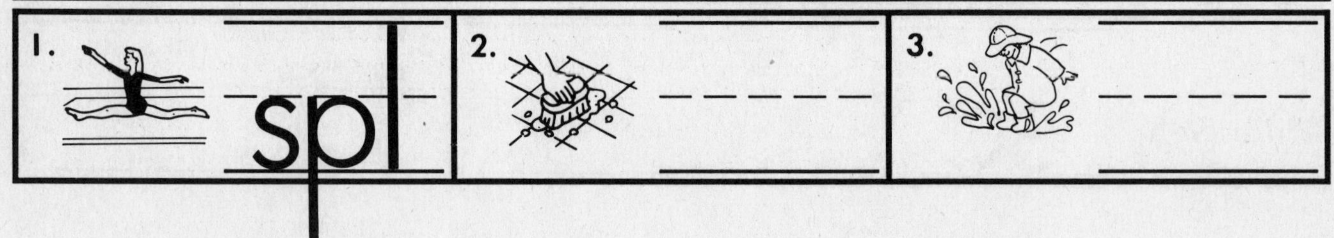

The word spray begins with the sound of spr. Say the name of each picture. If the name begins with the sound of spr, print spr in the box

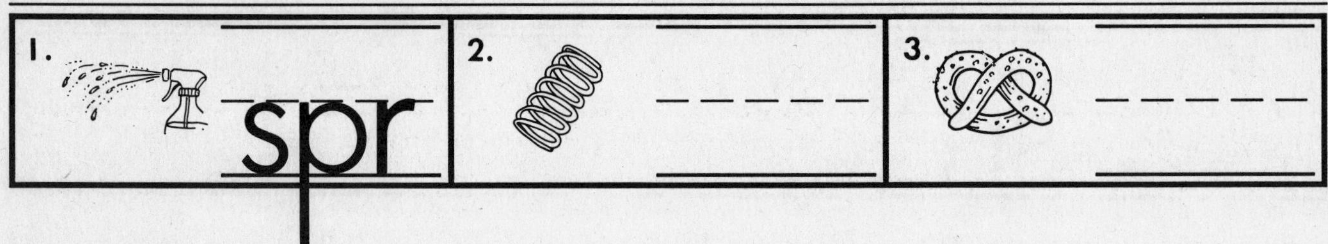

The word square begins with the sound of squ. Say the name of each picture. If the name begins with the sound of squ, print squ in the box.

The word street begins with the sound of str. Say the name of each picture. If the name begins with the sound of str, print str in the box.

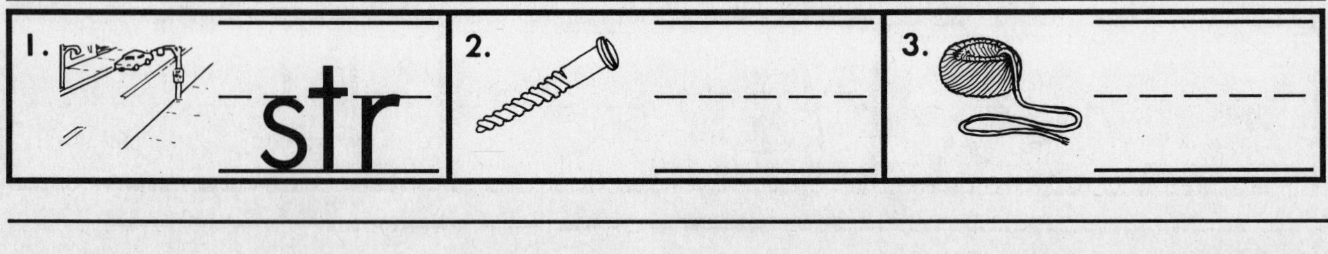

S Blends

Read the words that are part of a sentence. Circle the word that will finish the sentence. Print the word in the box.

1. Jack and Jill had fun on the slide.	slide slick stride
2. The flag has green ________.	stops stripes tribes
3. Dick will use a ________ to dig.	spill spade spray
4. Please, will you fix the ________?	skate Kate stripe
5. The steps are ________.	scream street steep
6. Sally can ________ a mile.	swim slim spin
7. The ________ is wide and clean.	scream scold street
8. Did you ________ the milk?	still spill splint

Y as a Vowel

Say the name of each picture. If the y at the end of the name has the long sound of i, print i in the box. If it has the long sound of e, print e in the box.

1.  i	2. 	3. 
4. 	5. 	6. 
7. 	8. 	9. 
10.  20	11. 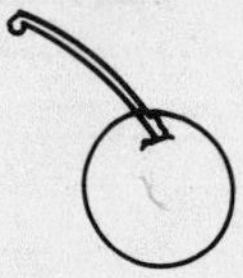	12.  50

Say the name of each picture. Circle its name.

1.  bunny baby buddy	2.  penny pony Polly	3.  bag bunny baby
4.  fry fly fan	5.  50 fifty fly fairy	6.  sky skin skill
7.  can candy cry	8.  puppy penny poppy	9.  city pony cry
10.  20 plenty twenty seventy	11.  fairy funny penny	12. 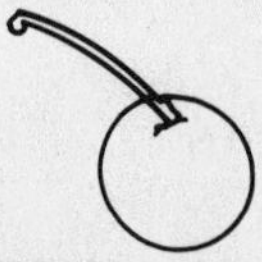 berry cheek cherry

Y as a Vowel

Say the name of each picture. Circle its name.

1.	2.	3.
cap cry can carry	fly fry fan fat	sty spy sky sly
4.	5.	6.
baby bake daddy carry	baby bug buddy bunny	poke pony pole penny

Say the name of each picture. Print its name in the box.

1.	2.	3.
baby		
4.	5.	6.

Y as a Vowel

Look at the picture. Circle the word that will finish the sentence. The word you pick will be the name of the picture. Print the word in the box.

1.	Polly likes to ride the pony.	penny, poppy, pony
2.	We ate a ______ pie.	berry, penny, bunny
3.	Teddy is a happy ______.	bunny, baby, puppy
4.	Dolly looked up at the blue ______.	cry, sky, skill
5.	My ______ is funny.	berry, penny, bunny
6.	I ride a bus in the ______.	city, poppy, penny
7.	I picked a ______ from the tree.	funny, monkey, cherry
8.	The ______ is on the wall.	fly, fifty, cry

Consonant Digraph: TH

The word thumb begins with the sound of th. Say the name of each picture. If the name begins with the sound of th, print th in the box.

1. 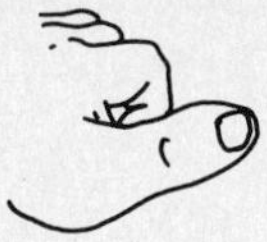 th	2. 	3. 
4.  13	5. 	6.  10
7. 	8. 	9. 
10.  3	11. 	12.  30

Say the name of each picture. Circle its name.

1.  thumb thin numb	2.  throng throne tone	3.  trick track truck
4.  thank think drink	5.  trap trade drape	6.  3 three tree free
7.  three free tree	8.  cloth teeth faith	9.  wind math moth
10.  thimble rumble trim	11.  plank thank theater	12.  path bath bat

Consonant Digraph: WH

The word white begins with the sound of wh. Say the name of each picture. If the name begins with the sound of wh, print wh in the box.

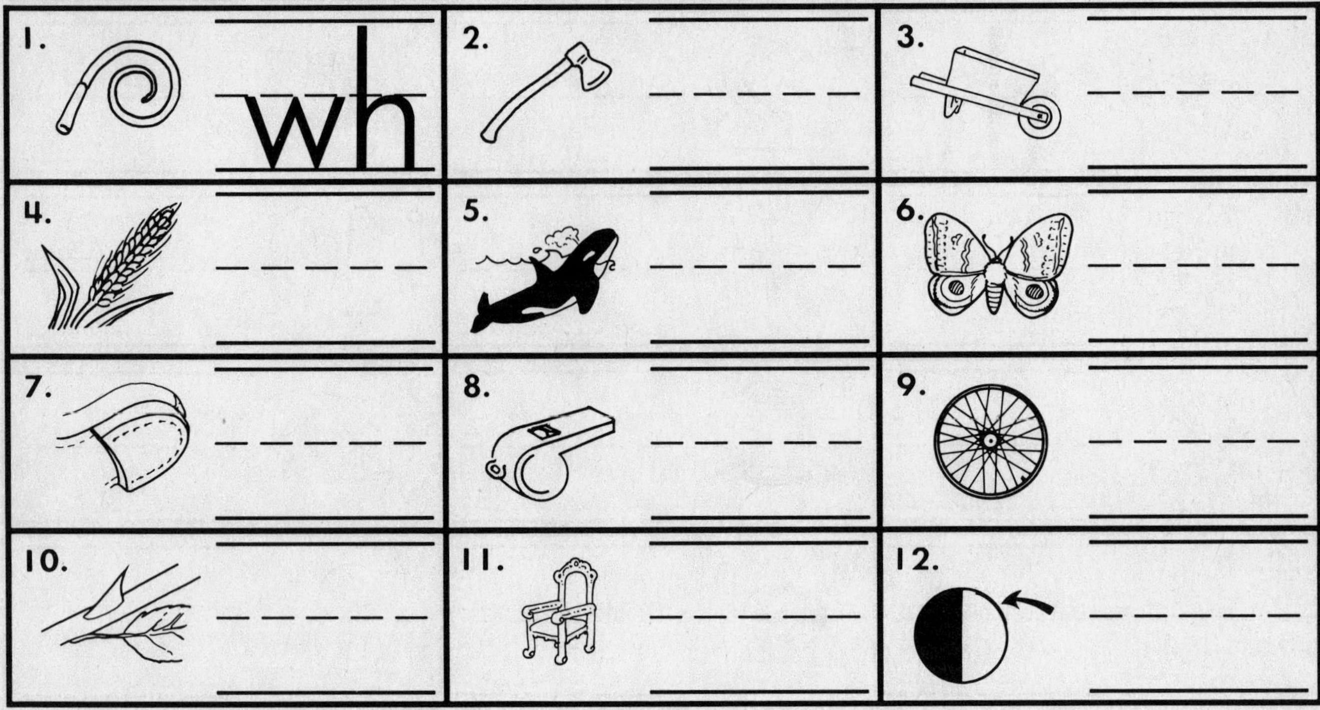

Say the name of each picture. Circle its name.

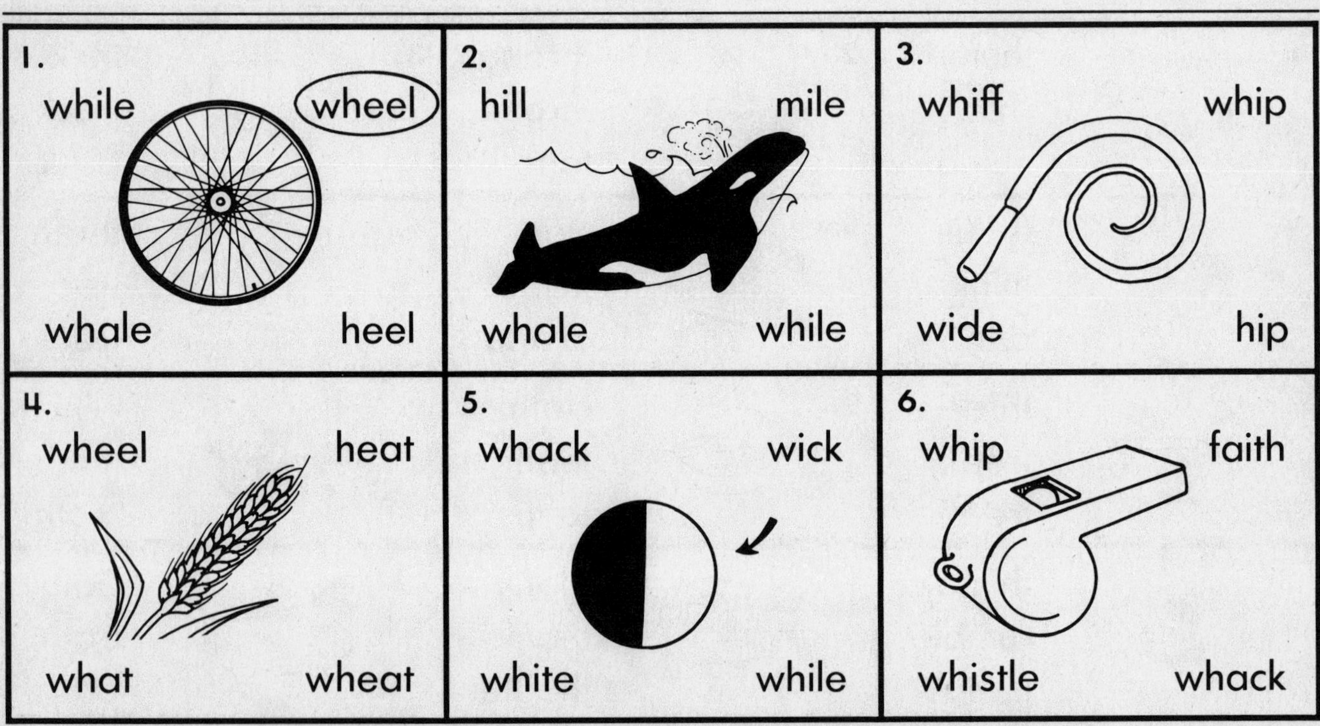

Consonant Digraph: SH

The word ship begins with the sound of sh. Say the name of each picture. If the name begins with the sound of sh, print sh in the box.

1. sh	2.	3.
4.	5.	6.
7.	8.	9.
10.	11.	12.

Say the name of each picture. Circle its name.

1. shoe blue shop	2. smile soak smoke	3. sleep sheep sheet
4. fresh flash fish	5. shade shape shake	6. spade spin spine
7. self shelf shell	8. shy sip ship	9. sell shall shell
10. brush crush rush	11. fish dish wish	12. shoe wish shirt

Consonant Digraph: CH

The word chair begins with the sound of ch. Say the name of each picture. If the name begins with the sound of ch, print ch in the box.

1.  ch	2. 	3 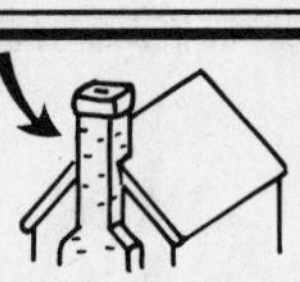
4. 	5. 	6. 
7. 	8. 	9. 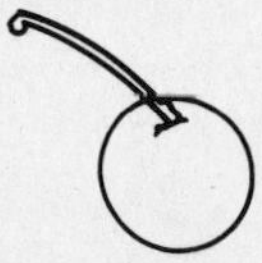
10. 	11. 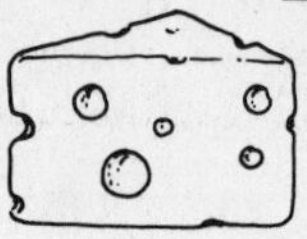	12. 

Say the name of each picture. Circle its name.

1.  chicks clicks licks	2.  chess chip chest	3.  peach each teach
4. 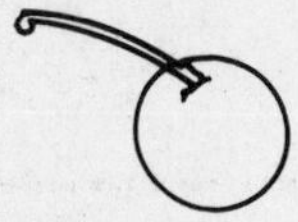 share merry cherry	5.  chick check shock	6. 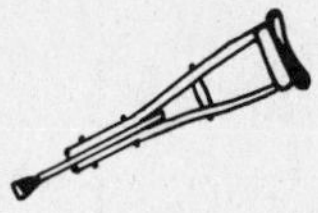 club crutch crush
7.  path patch mash	8.  cheer cherry share	9.  share plain chain
10.  chain share chair	11.  couch mouth cash	12.  shin chin shine

Consonant Digraphs

Say the name of each picture. Circle its name.

1. whale white snail while	2. why white whip wick	3. shame shot chin chain
4. what shone throat throne	5. chip chop ship shop	6. tease sheet teeth teach
7. chill chime shall shell	8. white wheel when weed	9. what wheat why cheat
10. three thirty wheat she	11. shocks shacks chicks checks	12. chair champ she shade

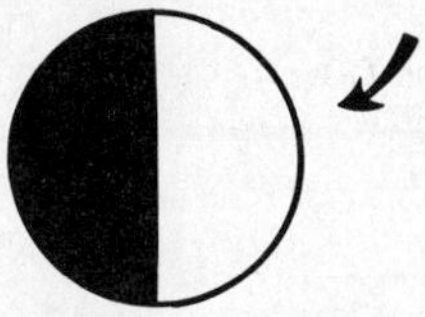

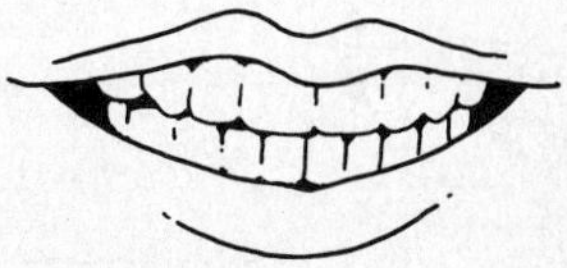

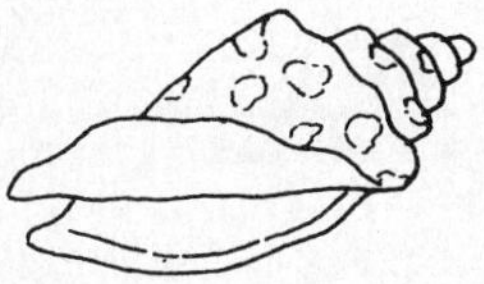

Consonant Digraphs

Read the words that are part of a sentence. Finish the sentence by writing the words from the box in the correct order.

1. Tom has seen a white moth.	a white moth
2. When will ____________?	sail ship the
3. I think the dog ____________.	bath a needs
4. We filled the ____________.	with shells box
5. Set the dish ____________.	this on shelf
6. I gave the seed ____________.	to the chicks
7. My bike has ____________.	wheel bent a
8. Give the team ____________.	big a cheer